IT'S NOT PERSONAL

BUILD YOUR BUSINESS LIKE A BOSS WITH WINNING ADVICE FROM A CEO

ROBERT VARAKIAN

ISBN: 978-1-66786-234-7 (paperback)

ISBN: 978-1-66786-235-4 (ebook)

CONTENTS

PART 1

MOB QUOTES

INTRODUCTION

Our culture has long been fascinated with gangsters, the Mob, the Mafia, the Cosa Nostra, whatever you call it.

The movies made of the various characters have become beloved classics.

What you may not know is that, despite the lack of formal education or the seemingly stupid moves some of these mobsters have made over the years, their stories, and their quotes (real and celluloid), offer amazing insight into how you can approach everyday practical matters of business, and they prove far more entertaining than your average business book. You just need to add the common sense of how to manage people and your business.

Godfather or CEO?

Captains or corporate VP?

Rules or policy and procedure?

Oath of loyalty or non-compete contracts?

Rub outs or layoffs?

The family or the company?

Respect or obey the rules?

Boss of all bosses or chairman of the board?

The five families or the conglomerate?

DONE YET?

**"I'll handle it, I told you I can handle it,
I'll handle it."**

Michael Corleone, *The Godfather*

Music to a boss's ear. Don't listen to the old army story about never volunteering for anything. Or the story about how they asked for volunteers and everyone but you took a step backwards. If you see an opportunity, grab it. It may not come around again.

There once was a marketing manager who witnessed not one, but two VP sales and marketing executives in his mid-sized company exit the company within a short period of time, leaving the company without a VP of sales or marketing. The president, who was fairly new to the company, explained to the young marketing manager that he was going to hire someone new and hoped to get a more strategic-thinking person for the job. This new hire would, of course, also become the young marketing manager's boss and may or may not be good for his career. The marketing manager wound up with the job and actually kept his original duties as marketing manager plus did the job of BOTH sales and marketing VPs.

How? The answer is in the next section.

MEMO TO MANAGEMENT

When you take on additional responsibility or any project, make sure you know when you are expected to provide updates. Bosses HATE to not know or to have to chase down people for follow up. It's a pleasure to give someone on your staff a project when you KNOW it will get done, and you KNOW they will update you on the progress and the completion. It SUCKS to have to continually ask and for people to promise a response by a certain date, and that date comes and goes and there's crickets. I fired someone for continually giving me dates for updates and continually missing them. If he had just said, "I told you I'd have it by this date, but I need more time," it would not have been as bad as being ignored with a total lack of follow up.

THE GODFATHER OF
GODFATHER ADVICE

"I'm going to make him an offer he can't refuse."

Don Corleone, *The Godfather*

Remember the marketing manager that wound up with the vice president's job?

He made an offer that the president of the company couldn't refuse.

He told the president that he would continue to do his current job and the job of both the departed VPs of sales and marketing for no additional increase in salary. He did not want a raise until he could prove his worth and prove he would do the job well. Once the president was convinced at some point in the future, the president could pay him what he felt was fair compensation.

Now, the president was new and did not know the marketing manager that well, and the marketing manager needed to offer his rationale for why he felt he could do it. He had to make a convincing pitch for the opportunity, despite never holding a sales position at any company. The president was intrigued but not completely sold, so he agreed to it as an interim position and would announce it that way. He explained that, if it failed, the marketing manager could exit without losing too much face, and if it worked, the president would announce it as a permanent position. The marketing manager was prepared to get by on two hours of sleep if needed to make it work. He did cut down on sleep and worked his tail off. He got the position and the raise within six months and went on to lead the company to new heights.

I was that marketing manager.

MEMO TO MANAGEMENT

Keep one thing in mind, once you take the noble step of taking on more responsibility: you will ruin virtually all that goodwill if you ever complain about being too busy, especially if you volunteered for the additional work. Go ahead, be macho and take the extra work, just don't wimp out. And for crying out loud, don't turn in a half-baked effort. You should realize your gesture has given you increased visibility—don't blow it. Produce something to be proud of.

TIGHTWADS AND PENNY PINCHERS

**"The soldiers don't want him; he squeezes
a quarter until the eagle screams."**

John Gotti, *Gotti*

I have a firm rule that if you work for a company, you should always treat the company's money as you would your own. Don't ever be wasteful or a big shot on someone else's dime—it is bad form.

I believe in business class travel for overseas flights. But an employee should not be able to simply pick the flight that suits their frequent flyer number if it is going to cost an extra bundle of cash. The flip side of that is you, as the boss, should not force an employee to take a crazy series of connections with long layovers and ridiculous arrival times to save $200 either. I have seen both extremes.

Crazy connections on overseas flights increase the odds of a missed flight or a late arrival that can throw off the schedule of a two-week trip pretty quickly, as well as make the executive so exhausted on arrival. The productivity takes a dip, so there is always a tradeoff. If you can arrange a reasonable flight schedule and reasonable connections, you should always book the cheaper flight.

Travel is not easy and rarely glamorous, even though people in the company who don't travel think it's a big party. I also think it's good to review the itinerary of travel before approving the trip. If it's not deemed productive enough, don't take the trip. If you are not flying in a sensible manner, rearrange the trip. I knew a sales VP who would zigzag back and forth across the country instead of taking a sensible approach to geographic planning. I have also seen people traveling to Asia spend several nights in Hong Kong hotels when the factories are in China, thereby tripling the cost of hotels. That practice was quickly stopped.

One exception for me is entertaining customers. If you are bringing them to a Knicks game, splurge for the seat on the floor in celebrity row (assuming it's a valued customer). The customer will NEVER forget it, and you reap that goodwill for years. Go with cheap seats and you are better off not going.

If you are entertaining a customer where there will be drinking, insist on providing the customer with a car service on your dime. Everyone will be more relaxed, have a few more drinks, and arrive home safely. The gesture goes a long way toward having a better time and will be appreciated by the customer as well as their spouse.

MEMO TO MANAGEMENT

I made two trips for two different bosses at two different companies. One was a two-and-a-half-week trip working weekends, etc. The flight schedules the company-appointed travel agency gave me had me arriving home in the middle of the night in the middle of a holiday weekend to save $1,000. The CEO would not approve an earlier flight so I could get home to family at a reasonable hour and at the beginning of the holiday weekend.

The other trip was three weeks overseas to develop and finalize product that was going to be shown at a trade show in San Francisco. I flew directly to the show from Asia with the last-minute samples. I managed to get everything done with three weeks of solid hard work. At the conclusion of the trade show, my boss flew my wife out to San Francisco and sent us to wine country for a few days on the company's dime. He did this to show his appreciation for my effort.

Which boss are you going to run through a wall for?

KNOWING WHO GETS PAID FIRST

"Take that money off the bar, nobody pays for nothing when they're with me."

Tough Tony Mira demanding that Donnie Brasco take his cash off the bar, *Donnie Brasco*

Some private equity (PE) firms operate as bottom feeders, often buying troubled firms. They strip all costs out and try to get a quick turnaround on their investment. They feel there are always deeper cuts available with a more ruthless approach than perhaps the former management team did not or would not take. Payments to creditors, staff, and others can become quite tight, and, often, the finance department and CEO need to make tough decisions when cash flow becomes tight. Often, it is the supplier payments that get stretched and delayed. Suppliers are sometimes given a fictional account of what is really going on. Unfortunately, sometimes, the more patient suppliers get hurt the most as they settle for a portion of every dollar due. The suppliers that stop shipping the earliest, until their account is made whole, often come out in the best shape.

Mob accounts, or restaurants and bars that were making Mob payments, often found that Mob guys would use these places as their frequent hangout locations and never pay for anything. In many cases, the restaurant owner was paying the Mob Boss a fee or percent of the gross, and erroneously figured that was the full amount he had to pay—not considering the free food and drink to the crew. The thing is, if the establishment suffers and has cash problems, the Mob Boss still gets his full cut, and it is paid on time, no matter what.

The private equity firm that invests in businesses in the hopes of turning them around for a quick profit does not care if they save jobs. In reality, they don't even care if the business survives after they sell it. But once they make their investment, the first thing that goes on the books is their monthly management fee. This fee is to be paid in full and on time, no matter what. (Sound familiar?) Payments to suppliers that actually provide the goods can be delayed. Deals can be worked out to pay them partial instead of full payment, even if it means losing a supplier. This is not the normal concern of the PE firm (unless the company can't live without that supplier). Other suppliers can usually be found, and the cycle starts anew, but that is left to management. The PE firm gets paid in full and on time or all hell breaks loose.

MEMO TO MANAGEMENT

Make sure the boss gets his first, whether it is his fee, his report, or an answer to his email.

SPECIALISTS PROSPER
MORE THAN GENERALISTS

There was a time when traveling salesmen were referred to as "bagmen," and this same term was applied to Mob associates, often to those carrying the loot. Women were sometimes used for these purposes, and a famous one was Virginia Hill. During a congressional hearing, she was questioned by New Hampshire Senator Charles Tobey, who asked,

"Young lady, what makes you the favorite of the underworld?"

Hill replied, "Senator, I'm the best goddamned lay in the world."

(The Mafia Encyclopedia)

In business, your sales "bagmen" come in two distinct varieties—the generalist and the specialist. The generalist is usually in charge of the specialist, much like the VP of sales is over the key account manager. In truth, the specialist is the much more valuable commodity, as the generalist is much easier to replace, and his or her loss generally inflicts less pain. If you are starting out in business, try and carve out a specialist's role for yourself, certainly not one like Virginia Hill, but something of significant value. It's better to be really good at one thing than just okay at a bunch of things, at least early in your career.

As a company president, I made one of the worst mistakes of my career (to this day), and all because I did not properly value one of our sales specialists. This person was the account manager for Wal-Mart, at the time our largest account. I placed too much value on our brand and product success and not enough on the importance of this specialist, namely his customer knowledge and relationship. The specialist wound up resigning after we had a tough phone call and went directly to our main competitor, who had been trying to steal the salesperson for months. Our business was critically harmed, and we did not regain the momentum we had had for quite some time. I regret the way I handled that phone call to this day. My lesson was learned the hard way: some people under your supervision need to be given more rope, and sometimes you have to swallow hard and live another day.

MEMO TO MANAGEMENT

Who in your organization performs a sales specialist role that, if they left and went to a competitor, it would hurt so much that you would regret it for years? Are they happy? Are you sure? And are they covered with a non-compete clause in the employment agreement?

PROTECT YOUR TURF

There was a particularly vile criminal named Pretty Ambergris in the early 1900s who was confronted by Dutch Shultz: "Pretty, I think I'm going to come in as your partner in Brooklyn."

Pretty replied, "Dutch, why don't you put a gun in your mouth and see how many times you can pull the trigger?"

(The Mafia Encyclopedia)

Pretty also had a habit of murdering customers who owed him money, but only the customers who owed him small amounts so he would not be out large sums of money, and this would send the message to those who owed him larger sums to prioritize the payments.

When Gillette first saw Harry's and other start-up blade companies pop up, I imagine there were several executives at Gillette who were not initially concerned and did not think a relook at their pricing strategy was worth the effort. They probably did not want to dip into their huge margins and felt it would blow over. I wonder if those executives are still employed at Gillette. This type of thing is more the norm now than the exception, especially with companies that start up with a direct-to-consumer internet strategy supported by radio advertising, often with the founder of the company making the pitch in plain talk and appealing to a new wave of consumers that are not that impressed by long standing national brands, traditional retail outlets, or celebrity pitchmen.

MEMO TO MANAGEMENT

Ignore nothing. The game has changed. Consumers with online consumer reviews now have the power to communicate as never before. Start-ups can create their own distribution strategy, and create appeal as outsiders, disrupters, whatever you want to call them. Every threat, even if it seems small or of little consequence, should be addressed. Develop a plan to address it (even if you never use it). Be prepared to react if you need to. This applies to product, processes, intellectual property, etc. Let the industry know that you will protect every inch of your turf and act quickly and ruthlessly. Make sure people will think twice before entering your arena.

WHEN TO KEEP QUIET

"Never let anyone know what you're thinking."

Don Corleone, *The Godfather*

The Don admonishes his son, Sonny, for speaking out of turn and letting his competitors gain an insight into his thinking, which is later used against him.

I often wonder why so many companies release product introduction information so far in advance of the date the product actually ships. It seems the only people who benefit from this information are the competition. I put a gag order on marketing managers talking to trade papers for this very reason.

There is no benefit to being an open book with your competitors.

While people should not be paranoid, it still amazes me how loose people are with how they talk, where they talk, and in front of whom they talk. I have overheard confidential business information from competitors while sitting next to them on the plane as they make calls to associates. I have overheard conversations in elevators, at restaurants and bars, and even in customers' lobbies while waiting for an appointment. You would think people would have more common sense, but they don't. I am amazed how freely people talk at trade shows when they KNOW the entire industry is there. The same goes for restaurants, bars, hotels, elevators—it never fails to amaze me, but it happens all the time.

I was traveling in Asia on a plane, and the man across the aisle from me was a designer traveling with a principal from one of his manufacturing facilities. The designer worked for one of my main competitors and had his entire new line sprawled out and was discussing all the critical points of the product over a few glasses of wine. I could not resist introducing myself, but only at the end of the flight. The flight attendant came over to lift his jaw off the floor.

While most people don't tell their customers or suppliers everything they are thinking, what you don't say can be as important, if not more so, than what you do say. Sometimes we give the quiet types the benefit of the doubt as being cerebral, perhaps more than they actually are in some cases. The following phrase is sometimes credited to Abraham Lincoln and sometimes to Mark Twain, "It is better to remain silent and be thought a fool, than to speak and remove all doubt."

A supplier asks you for a target price that you are looking to pay. Do you tell him a realistic price, shoot a lowball number, or plead the fifth? While it is rare that one answer works 100% of the time, personally, I don't believe in giving the target price, as it seems the first person who throws out the number generally weakens his position. You can always counter the actual quote, and there is the chance your target may be higher than what they were going to quote in the first place, so why take the chance?

How about at your own place of employment? How much do you trust your fellow workers to tell them what you are thinking? Even after you remove politics, religion and sex as off limits, how much do you tell coworkers what you think of your job, your boss, your other coworkers, etc.? Water cooler gossip can back up like a constipated mule, so be careful. Eventually, the mule gets over it, and when it explodes, everyone gets dirty. Even friends become ex-friends, or vengeful terminated employees, or just can't keep their mouths shut. You don't want to be in a position of having your career derailed because someone repeated something you should not have said in the first place.

Have you ever heard of anyone telling a coworker their great idea and then that coworker passing it off as their own idea? Of course, it happens all the time. So a modified version of the Don Corleone quote can be:

"Never tell anyone what you're thinking if the timing isn't right."

You need to make sure you have the right audience, and that audience needs to be in a receptive mood at the time you tell them your thoughts. If you've spent time creating brilliance, spend another moment to make sure your timing is correct.

MEMO TO MANAGEMENT

As a business leader, your staff needs to know exactly what you are thinking when it comes to strategic direction and priorities for the company, the staff, and their individual departments. Associates hate it when leaders are not clear on expectations and priorities. Don't waste their time by not properly and clearly communicating what needs to be done, what you expect to be done, and when you expect it to happen. Quantify expectations when possible. I prefer priorities to be jointly developed on an annual basis and signed off by staff and management. They should be reviewed monthly to check progress toward the quantifiable goal. The expected result needs to have accountability, with the possibility of adjusting the priorities pending unforeseen circumstances. I also like the idea of reviewing all departments' priorities together in a staff meeting so each area is clear on what the other departments are prioritizing and how they are progressing.

INTEGRITY COUNTS

**"They don't rat, why? That's the rule.
You don't break, you don't rat, basic rules."**

John Gotti, *Gotti*

Take the high road or be prepared to take the highway.

Don't try to build yourself up by tearing someone else down—it only makes you look small. The exception is if you have first-hand knowledge of something illegal or unethical, then it is your duty to talk. Just be sure you are 100% certain you know what you are talking about.

But barring an illegal or unethical activity, resist the urge to shovel dirt. You don't want to be the office gossip, and every office has a few. It is not your job to be the commentary associate passing judgment on everyone's qualifications, work habits, lifestyles, and performance. Sometimes people say things in meetings that make you want to rip their heads off. Perhaps they just threw you under the bus. You don't have to remain silent; you can call them on it, but do it calmly and with facts, and try to be as non-confrontational as possible. I realize it is not easy.

A song lyric from the Jefferson Starship goes – "are you saying something you know or just repeating something you heard?" Keep that in mind if you are tempted to pass along something you heard, that maybe, just maybe, it's not even true. How would you feel if it turns out to be untrue and damages some-one's reputation?

The rules are simple:

If it involves someone's personal life, leave it alone. That is why it is called personal.

If it involves the way they go about their job or conduct them-selves, leave it that person's boss to handle. You are not the cav-alry. Unless it is directly impacting your performance, I suggest going to that person directly for a conversation, not a written diatribe.

MEMO TO MANAGEMENT

You are no longer one of the boys. A company president I knew continued to have regular lunch dates with a group of staff two levels down from his position, basically socializing with the direct reports of HIS direct reports, and flapped his gums about various personnel, which of course was repeated and attributed to the company president, ensuring a lack of respect for this president throughout the organization. The further up you ascend on the food chain, the more circumspect you should become with your comments.

GET OVER YOURSELF

"Did you go to college to get stupid?"

Sonny Corleone talking to his brother, Michael, *The Godfather*

An MBA is a fine and wonderful item to have in one's possession. Just don't fall in love with yourself for having one. There are more than a few Harvard MBAs (nothing against Harvard, just making a point) I have come across who failed miserably at various jobs that people with lesser degrees (or no degree) excelled at. If you have managed to secure an MBA, congratulations. You deserve a tip of the cap for being dedicated enough to stick to it and complete your assignments to a level that secured you a degree. To the people without the advanced degree, or any degree for that matter, don't be in awe of your degree-laden coworkers. A degree or an MBA DOES help you get in the door and does increase your knowledge base, but you still need to be able to navigate the room. Performance is all that counts, and if you outperform others, you win—if you don't you lose. I once had a marketing VP that I inherited when I became CEO of a small gift company, and she made sure to list every one of her degrees (and she had a few) on her business card. The fact that she was a business lightweight and couldn't perform at her job was another story, but her business card went on forever—personally not a fan of that practice.

MEMO TO MANAGEMENT

Don't overlook the hard-working, performance-driven staff simply because they don't have a degree. In a company I ran that had four marketing VPs, three of them had MBAs, and the fourth, as it turned out, did not even have an undergraduate degree. The woman without the degree ran rings around the three MBAs, and to this day, is the only one of the four I would hire again. That doesn't mean degrees don't have value, they do; it just means the person matters more than the paper.

CLASS VS. CRASS

"It's the old-timer's style, you don't flash nothing."

Gotti associate, Neil Dellacroce, *Gotti*

This is a bit like Goofus and Gallant, except it was entertaining clients at two actual business dinners, and I was at both. My boss at the time, a different individual at each dinner, was paying the bill.

The large group of people were finishing up a great meal, talking and laughing loudly after consuming many bottles of fine wine. It looked like a success as our business clients enjoyed themselves; the food, the wine, the conversation. All was good and would probably help pave the way for a friendly business relationship going forward. When the waiter brought the bill to the table, my boss reached for it and began to loudly say how expensive it was, how much the wine cost, etc. The evening screeched to a halt, and the customers looked aghast. I felt like crawling under the table. The goodwill of the dinner seemed to evaporate, and I am sure the customers' takeaway was what a boob their host was.

Another time, another large group of people were finishing up a spectacular meal with great conversation and many bottles of fine wine. The host for this particular meal was a different person from the first example. He discreetly signaled the waiter for the bill after making sure that there were no further requests from the table. His request for the bill, his receipt of the bill, and the way he signed the bill in silence and in his lap went totally unnoticed by everyone at the table. They just continued their conversation uninterrupted until we left the restaurant. No one had any idea he paid or how much it cost. The only thing they noticed was how much of a good time they had.

MEMO TO MANAGEMENT

People already know you are the boss, you already have the power, and everyone knows it. No need to remind them or to yell, berate, or act like a boob. My personal mentor never raised his voice, never cursed, never criticized you in front of a group. He never demanded respect; he just earned it by being a gentleman and role model and treating people fairly. This did not mean he was a pushover; he fired people who deserved to be fired and did it quickly, quietly, and never denigrated them on their way out the door.

DON'T BE A STRANGER

"Now you come to me and you say, Don Corleone, give me justice, but you don't ask with respect, you don't offer friendship, you don't even think to call me Godfather."

Don Corleone, *The Godfather*

Do you have any "convenient friends," people who are your friends at opportune times (opportune for them)? While they may not realize it, this is always transparent. Networking is not reaching out when you need something. Networking is staying in touch when there is no apparent reason driving your reaching out. Then, when the time comes when you might need some information, a reference, a job, or whatever assistance you need, it will be much easier to make an approach with dignity. On the flip side of that is how you respond to the other person when they are seeking something from you. Do you go out of your way to help, or do you do the minimum to just get rid of them? Do you REALLY help or just pass the buck? It feels good to help people, even if it never gets repaid. If someday you need the help, all the better.

MEMO TO MANAGEMENT

In life, or business, when you say to someone that you will get back to them by such and such date with such and such information, make damn sure you follow up and produce. If, for some reason, you can't meet the date or the requirements of what you promised, get back to them and tell them why. Let them know when you will complete what you promised to complete. Failing to follow up on what you promised is one of the biggest personal blunders anyone can make, and believe me, the other person remembers— for a long, long time.

WHO IS ON THE SOAPBOX?

**"Let him talk, don't interrupt,
and don't dare underestimate him."**

Neil Dellacroce, advising John Gotti before a meeting with the Boss
Don Carlo, *Gotti*

Ego is such a large part of business. Many bosses are Type A driven personalities with substantial egos. Even people with little to no ego hate to be interrupted, but people with power and egos REALLY hate to be interrupted. The CEO (Godfather) expects respect, expects people to be quiet until they are finished talking, and expects people's full attention while they are talking (put the phone down). Most people like to hear themselves talk. Granted, there are some exceptions. Bosses and customers like to be heard and generally feel their words are full of inspiring wisdom. This is reinforced since people rarely disagree with either the boss or the customer. Your interruption of their sermon could indicate that you don't value their opinion as much as they do.

MEMO TO MANAGEMENT

This advice goes up exponentially the larger the group. When you are in a one-on-one setting, people are generally more open to a frank conversation and a respectful difference of opinion. However, when in a large group, you need to really be careful if you are putting anyone on the spot or challenging their position, especially if they are a customer or your boss. The other thing many people seem to forget is when to shut up. Once you have made your point, especially if it goes over fairly well, be quiet. If you keep talking, you could either lose the victory of the point you just made or aggravate people by coming across as if you are trying to rub in just how brilliant you are.

YOU CAN PICK YOUR FRIENDS

"It's Cosa Nostra, we got the boss we got."

Sammy Gravano, *Gotti*

You can pick your friends, but not your family and often not your boss.

Most people have had at least one boss that drove them bat crazy—some have had nothing but bosses that drove them bat crazy.

Who can you complain to? Really just your spouse, and it reminds me of a good Chris Rock joke. Goes something like this:

"Every man has heard his wife complain about "that woman" at work, how horrible she is, how lazy she is, how sloppy she is, how inconsiderate she is, and one day I made the mistake after listening to a story about what happened that day. I said 'Well, maybe she had a point, I could see why she did that.' And after the look I got from my wife and the subsequent tirade, I learned there is only one appropriate response I can give, and it's, "That bitch, how could she?"

So when you want to complain about your boss, keep your comments to your spouse, and when your spouse complains about their boss, keep your reply to, "That bitch, how could she?" maybe over a glass of wine or two, and all will be fine.

MEMO TO MANAGEMENT

Complaining about your boss to your coworkers is dangerous ground. Your coworkers may one day get promoted themselves, no longer be friendly with you, be up for the same promotion you are, or begin to date the boss (it happens). If you are in a company where groups of people socialize, where there is drinking, be extra careful what you say after a few cocktails. When others talk, let them, and try to be as unresponsive as possible.

WHACK ATTACK

"Nobody is going to get whacked unless
the Boss of this family approves, understand."

Paul Castellano, *Gotti*

Many executives have authority to hire and fire their staff as they see fit, which is entirely understandable, and also desirable, and in some cases, insisted upon. Great, I get it, congratulations. You da man.

Sometimes you might be pulling the trigger on someone who was with the company long before you arrived on the scene. Maybe you did not know that person was once the personal assistant to the CEO, and the CEO has a soft spot for them. Or maybe they are the third cousin once removed from the CEO's wife.

Maybe they are some sort of legacy like Flounder from Animal House.

But you da man, and you are in charge of your domain and can hire and fire at your discretion for your department.

The safe approach is to be like Paul Castellano and discuss it with your boss—even if you DO have the authority, and even if the person is not Flounder, or the third cousin of his wife once removed, and even if he really deserves to be fired. Bosses appreciate being kept in the loop. If the boss has an issue, they will tell you and hopefully it is something that can be worked out, but better to discuss it upfront to be sure. If it is just a quick rubber stamp "Okay" from your boss, he or she probably appreciated the heads up anyway.

MEMO TO MANAGEMENT

Make sure you know how to "manage up" as well as how you "manage down." Realize one of the big issues for most CEOs is being isolated and being the last to know. Don't pass on every inane detail of your life and waste your boss's time. If you can determine what type of issues or information they want you to pass up, once you do that and keep them informed at the level THEY want to be informed, you become a more valued associate.

WHEN YOU NEED TO SAY GOODBYE

**"What a life, pal'n around with the guy
I'm going to have clipped."**

John Gotti, *Gotti*

Okay, so now you are the boss. While no one wants to be an island, how do you conduct yourself with the rest of the company, particularly if you were promoted from within and had preexisting relationships with other associates? Touchy subject.

It is not necessary to be friends, and it's better if you're not. You can be friendly, but professional, which means never over-sharing personal information. Your goal is to be respected, not liked. If you turn out to be liked, consider it a bonus.

Everyone who works for you is under evaluation. If they don't perform, you may need to remove them, no matter their personal situation or how likeable they are—don't forget it.

Sometimes you will find yourself in social situations with your staff, at a bar, on a company trip, etc. A good rule of thumb is don't be among the last to leave; better to leave earlier than later. Give your staff a chance to unwind without you and talk more freely. By showing up and buying a round or two, you did your good deed, and then you should leave. The last thing you want is drunken boss stories floating around the office.

MEMO TO MANAGEMENT

The sobering part of John Gotti's comment is the reality of it. Eventually you are going to have to fire someone that you have traveled with, had good times with, and probably like as a person. Maybe you have met their family and know their struggles or personal challenges and goals. It's not easy. In fact, it's damn hard. Don't make it more difficult by talking too much about stuff you should have kept to yourself. The last thing you want is a terminated employee armed with information about you, the company, or its associates that should have been kept confidential. Inside your brain, there should be a shut-off valve for dispensing too much information.

TAKE STOCK

John Gotti, in prison asking an inmate, "Where'd you get the prosciutto?"

Answer, "I know people."

Gotti

In prison, prosciutto is inventory.

Inventory, no matter what it is, is cash.

If you don't realize that and act accordingly, you are not doing your job.

If you allow your sales force a large say in how inventory is managed without proper checks and balance, you may not deserve your job. And if you don't tie a reasonable portion of the salespersons' compensation to the positive results of that inventory management, you may not keep your job if the inventory drains you dry.

So, inventory is money, and how you manage that money depends on who you know, what they know, and what they tell you; or better yet, what you make them tell you. When you're hungry, it's good to know how much prosciutto there is, when it arrived, how old it is, and what other people are willing to pay for it.

Managing inventory is not the most exciting part of the business, and CEOs going through thousands of lines of data is not going to happen, so it is imperative to develop a few forms that keep it to the point and at a high enough level to be manageable by the CEO so he knows what is going on.

MEMO TO MANAGEMENT

If you develop only a single inventory form, at least have a solid "aged inventory" report. It's an eye opener when you list aged inventory in descending value of days on hand without a purchase order. It creates an interesting conversation when the CEO looks at the report and asks why we have this item in stock to the tune of 10,000 units when we have not had a customer purchase order for that product in 18 months. Also, there should be an in-depth cross departmental SKU rationalization process twice a year to keep things in check.

BLOOD BANKS

"I don't like violence, Tom. I'm a businessman, blood is a big expense."

Sollozo speaking to Tom Hagan, *The Godfather*

Different people treat employee turnover in different manners. Jack Welch had his famous (infamous) letting go of whoever scored in the lowest 20% of employee reviews each year. At this point, most people would not be on board with that approach. In fact, the entire review process is under siege by many as not productive.

Do whatever you can to minimize employee turnover. It is much more expensive than any study will show. Trained, knowledgeable, experienced, dedicated employees are your greatest asset. Don't ever take a chainsaw mentality to your business if you have any interest in keeping your business. For one thing, the cold hard numbers are hard to ignore: headhunter fees, relocation costs, severance packages, legal fees, and lawsuits.

In addition, bringing in people from the outside often requires higher salaries, not to mention what creating significant uncertainty does to the morale of your existing workforce. Then, due to brain drain, there is lost productivity from training, added ramp-up time, and strained customer and supplier relationships. Plus, sometimes the shine on the resume of the new person you just hired doesn't match the reality.

MEMO TO MANAGEMENT

Make sure you know your employees at a minimum of two levels below your level. Don't rely of filtered reports of personnel or canned employee evaluation reports. Attend certain staff meetings, and make sure people at various levels get to speak or make presentations at meetings you attend. Ask them to prepare and present a special project to give them an opportunity to spread their wings in front of you—let's see who can fly.

DO I STAY OR DO I GO NOW?

"Leave the gun, take the cannoli."

Clemenza, *The Godfather*

How often you leave a job and how you handle leaving a job are critical components of most careers. The last thing any prospective employer wants to see on a resume is a series of quick stops at each job as if you only stopped there long enough to fill the tank and change tires before getting back in the race. The flip side is not any better, especially if you are not showing strong continuous growth at your present company. If you are with Borax Inc. for 20 years without strong continuous advancement, most employers get the "bump on a log" impression. A lifelong participant of one system only knows how that system operates and generally has only one point of view.

I had a marketing manager tell me she was leaving to work for another company that offered her $80,000 (she was currently at

$70,000). I did not make a strong attempt to keep her and was somewhat offended when she offered to stay if I beat their offer of $80,000 by an additional $10,000. In essence, she was telling me her loyalty to the company was such that she wouldn't even stay if we paid her the same as the highest current offer she had. She would only stay if we beat it. I wished her good luck. I would not advise anyone to handle a move this way. Suppose you tell your boss you are leaving for a better offer and the boss counters, and you accept and decide to stay. I think there is always some level of unease after that.

MEMO TO MANAGEMENT

> Studies have shown people who make between three and five career moves have higher salaries than those who stay put in one place too long. When you do change jobs, consider the gun and the cannoli. You can't take anything illegal or steal confidential secrets, but the best thing you can take is your list of contacts, assuming it is okay to do so. Contacts for suppliers, associates, customers, and support staff could all come in useful at a later date.

BAD APPLE

"Paulie sold out the old man, that little strutz. I don't want to see him again. Make that first thing on your list, understand?"

Sonny Corleone, *The Godfather*

Negative situations need to be addressed quickly, and action needs to be clearly spelled out. The worst thing during a crisis is a lack of leadership or communication.

If the negative situation is an internal personnel situation, get rid of the bad apple quickly to save the barrel.

If there is a legal situation, make sure staff knows what they can and cannot do, what they can and cannot say, and who will handle the communications.

All steps in the crisis should be documented with action plans. Personnel responsible for each specific action need to be identified. Each action item needs a timeline. When each action item is completed, it needs to be confirmed. It is better to overcommunicate than undercommunicate.

If a corrective action plan can address the employee or situation, it needs to have a timeline for a date of review and a stay/go decision within that timeline pending specific corrective actions and results.

A list of both internal and external parties needs to be identified regarding who needs to be notified—government recalls and such have specific requirements. If it is not a government-mandated issue but an internal one, decide who is best to deal with customers and suppliers to minimize the damage.

MEMO TO MANAGEMENT

Sonny did several things correctly in his management directive. Number one, he acted quickly and decisively. Number two, he helped set his employees' priorities by telling them to make this action number one on their list. And number three, he was clear in stating what he wanted—there was no confusing the message. And finally, he asked for confirmation, "understand?"

FAVOR OF THE MONTH

"Just remember that I did you a favor."

Vito Corleone, *The Godfather II*

Throughout your career, and more importantly throughout your life, you will be on the receiving end of more than a few favors, some large, some small. Like Blanche in *A Streetcar Named Desire*, many people will depend on the kindness of strangers, not to mention friends, coworkers, bosses, staff, and relatives. The key word in Vito's quote is REMEMBER.

It is damn near impossible to get ahead in this world without the help of others, but it is impossible to stay ahead without that help. No one can do it all on their own. Never forget the people who have helped you, whether the stock boy or the CEO.

When you do remember and are in a position to repay the favor, how you go about it is more important than actually doing it. If you grouse about it or give the appearance of doing it reluctantly or that it is a hassle for you, you negate the benefits of the action and probably cause more harm than good. The person will remember the attitude more than the fact that you repaid the favor. Be glad to help. Be sincerely glad to help.

MEMO TO MANAGEMENT

I knew a senior division president who worked for a large company for almost 20 years, and the one takeaway he had from his 20 years was that his boss never once said "thank you" or "job well done." It stuck in his craw forever. It does not take much to say thank you or job well done, and people appreciate it more than they let on. A thank you is a favor that lets people know you appreciate and notice their effort. While it is the smallest favor one can imagine and takes little effort, some people are too self-absorbed or mean to even make that small effort. The same CEO was telling another division president about some sales concerns for a particular product line within the executive's division, and the executive went on to explain the reasons as well as tout some other recent successes. The CEO's reply: "Not everything you have done has been bad."

IN AND OUT

"Just when I thought I was out, they sucked me back in."

Michael Corleone, *The Godfather III*

Are you involved or committed? How committed? What side of the breakfast plate are you on? You know the story of ham and eggs: the chicken was involved, but the pig was committed.

I had a marketing VP that was IN and OUT. She was "in" when she thought there was a personal benefit such as making a presentation to senior management about an exciting new product the company recently developed or to report on some sell-through success at a major retailer. But she was not so visible when there was less flattering news to deal with. After making one of her presentations, which was very well received, we began a national launch of a major product roll-out at one of the largest retailers in the US. Unfortunately, we were soon on the receiving end of a government product safety recall and had to pull the product off shelves, issue consumer statements, and so forth. Once we received notice of the recall, you practically had to look under her desk to find her. She shied away from all contact and acted as if this was someone else's problem to deal with. It told me everything I needed to know about this executive, and I never considered her for advancement again.

MEMO TO MANAGEMENT

I have what I call the "Parade Rule." If you are willing to lead the parade when the sun is shining, you have to be willing to also march in front when it's raining. One thing most bosses hate is the person who runs into the corner office with every bit of good news, but keeps anything bad so far below the radar that the boss is the last person to hear about it. Good news in most corporations seems to travel at the speed of lightning, and bad news tends to languish. I would always tell my staff that bad news should travel at warp speed; the good news can wait a bit. Bad news often requires immediate action. Just remember not to kill the messenger. Otherwise, you just reinforce the behavior you are trying to stop.

BALANCE

"A man that doesn't spend time with his family can never be a real man."

Don Corleone, *The Godfather*

Work-life balance today is more important than it has ever been.

Bring your kids to work day is an example. Heck, they even have bark at the park for bringing your dog to the baseball game.

Company culture is so critical to today's younger worker. You see it repeatedly mentioned in so many reviews on Glassdoor. It can include casual dress codes, summer hours on Fridays, work from home when you have a family commitment, dentist appointment, your kid's events, house construction, or deliveries. More and more companies are rightly understanding these issues and work around them as much as possible.

Some people probably abuse these perks, and it is so difficult to enforce and monitor them. I am not sure of the best way to even try. In general, if the performance of the individual is up to snuff, then I would not sweat it.

Not that employees should get the same leeway as the boss, but how your boss approaches his work-life balance probably acts as a barometer for the organization.

I have tried to schedule most of my personal activities after hours so as not to disrupt my work duties unless I absolutely must. I found a dentist who takes routine visits on Saturdays, and I schedule mundane things like haircuts on weekends or evenings. So, while I encourage staff to have a proper work-life balance and stress family values, it does bug me a bit when people constantly take off for things I know are easily handled after hours.

MEMO TO MANAGEMENT

> People should always ask their boss for permission to cut out early to see their kid's baseball game, visit someone in the hospital, etc., rather than trying to be sly about it. And the response from the boss should always be the same, "Don't worry about it, family comes first."

CHEST POUNDING

"John, you beat the government, you're supposed to walk away humble, you're not supposed to stand in front of the TV cameras crowing about it. Because it's going to come back in your face."

Sammy Gravano talking to John Gotti, *Gotti*

How humble should you be when you have good results to share or report?

As humble as you can possibly be. And make sure the credit gets shared. The term "team effort" should be part of the speech. Best to let the positive results speak for themselves. Also, if you go over the top in reporting good news for this quarter, and the results the following quarter are not so great, the audience who witnessed your boastful presentation will remember how you approached the good news when they are looking at the current bad numbers. I prefer to not give people any extra incentive for anger when presenting poor numbers. Low-key for both good and bad seems the best way to proceed.

At one point in my career, I did not follow my own advice. I was running a mid-size, family-owned private company. Several family members who were now on the Board of Directors had previously run the company at various times (none with any great degree of success, by the way). My tenure produced better results than any of the previous management teams or family members. During a board meeting, I was pleased to report the year ending numbers as the best in the history of the company, which was in existence for around 60 years. I thought it was a fairly big deal and would be received as great news. While they were very pleased with the results, the family member who ran the company directly before my tenure, who was now my direct boss, took exception to it. I miscalculated the effect of ego. He felt it was a reflection on him, and instead of being pleased in his decision to hire someone who produced positive results, he felt it was unfairly putting his tenure in a negative light. He expounded on it at the board dinner after a few glasses of wine, and though I tried to defend the presentation, it was useless. A positive turned into a negative.

MEMO TO MANAGEMENT

Before making any presentation, role play the part of the recipient and pick apart the numbers and anything that can stick out as a potential snake in the grass. Your boss generally will focus on areas that could be better, are underperforming, or wherever the numbers might seem "off." Rather than wait for them to bring it up, it is better to be proactive, point out each area where things could be better, and recap both the reason for the shortfall as well as the corrective action plan, timing, and expected result of such action plan. Also, if the numbers are off by one particular cause of action, make sure you know what the numbers would have been had this singular event been removed. If the base business is healthy and performing well but was impacted by a singular event, that is one thing. If the entire business across the board is in the crapper, that is another story. Hopefully the numbers are good, as it's simple to prepare a presentation when the results are strong. Perfuming a pig is an ordeal. If you are prepared with answers and have facts arranged in a clear manner, you can avoid losing control of the meeting.

CONFRONTATION VS. COOPERATION

"We got more money to make working with the other families than shutting them out."

Paul Castellano, *Gotti*

Microsoft wants their software everywhere, and Apple wants theirs to be a closed system. A branded company refuses all offers to supply private label product while another company makes it a core competency. One company with patented parts only uses those parts in its own finished goods while another company figures it performs better by supplying that part to the entire industry it competes with.

Do you treat your competitors as mortal enemies or as potential allies?

Do you look beyond your traditional customer base for business? Are there joint venture opportunities or licensing opportunities going untapped? Is there another use or market opportunity for your product? Perhaps your product or service would make a nice giveaway or gift with purchase for some other company to capitalize on. Is there a cross-merchandising opportunity with your brand and another brand?

Sometimes closing shop altogether makes the most sense. Years ago, Farberware was the leading stainless steel cookware in the US and was made in the Bronx, New York. They were struggling financially, had outdated equipment, and were having difficulty competing against imported product. But they had a strong brand name. The people who bought the company closed the Bronx-based manufacturing facility. Instead of relocating the manufacturing to Asia, they exited the business of manufacturing altogether. Instead, they licensed the Farberware name to companies that were already in the cookware business. They were now in the business of collecting royalties for the use of the Farberware brand. Decades later, the royalties are still coming in strong. They also licensed the Farberware brand to many other companies for various product categories. Some worked well, others not so much. They had a period of time when they had so many licensees that things got oversaturated, but they eventually cleaned that up. Today, Farberware is a collection of different companies producing different products under the Farberware brand and paying a royalty to the company that purchased the business when they were located in the Bronx.

The owners of the brand? No inventory, no manufacturing, no headaches, and no employees, except maybe the person who opens the royalty checks.

MEMO TO MANAGEMENT

Licensing your brand or service to another company with more expertise than you possess is a way to capitalize on potential extra income and expand your brand with minimal financial investment. Many have done it, and usually the consumer is not even aware that the brand is actually multiple companies. I learned the pitfalls and benefits of licensing your brand. One of the times it did not work for me was when I chose a company that the industry did not regard at the same quality level as the brand. It is a decision I wish I could get a mulligan on. It is critical when you license your brand that the company you choose to work with has the same commitment to your brand as you do, and that both of you are on the same page in terms of brand positioning, channels of commitment, quality level, and go to market strategy. Also, you need to maintain communication on progress and should, at minimum, have annual planning and status update meetings.

INNER CIRCLE OR IN-LAW?

**"Give him a living, but never discuss
the family business with him."**

Don Corleone, talking to his son about his daughter's husband,
The Godfather

I know of a large public company that, to an extent, was run like
a family business. It once was a small private family business
that grew into a large public company, and the family members
still held the seats of power.

The son, despite having limited qualifications, was made president of the entire company by his CEO father. To my knowledge,
no one else was considered for the position. When you invest in
a public company, you would like to think the company is more
interested in having the most qualified individuals running the
show versus a less qualified family member. Unfortunately, often that is not the case. Looking at the financial results of this
company, the profits could go from 20 million one year to 1 million the next, and the division presidents had bonus money one

year but not the next. The company president? His total income remained basically stable year to year despite company performance. The fact that shareholders roll with these punches is interesting. All of this was public information, but to my knowledge, no shareholders ever revolted.

Sometimes it is a son-in-law or other distant relative that gains the benefits of a familial connection. These appointments sometimes turn out to be overpaid and under-qualified, but rarely hard working. The person gains a position of some importance but rarely rises to the top of the flow chart. The lazy ones are happy to be in a position to coast rather than going on their own to earn their way. They are corporate examples of "give him a living but never discuss the family business with him."

MEMO TO MANAGEMENT

> Protecting the family is great for the family. The rest of the non-family staff know it's a slanted playing field. If you play on their field, you need to accept and not begrudge anyone or how they benefit. That's just life. Coming across as disingenuous undermines your credibility.

THIS DAMN INDECISION IS KILLING ME

"More is lost by indecision than by the wrong decision."

Tony Soprano, *The Sopranos*

Maybe, maybe not. It depends on the scope and potential impact, upside potential, downside risk, and all that jazz.

Being in a position with a boss that has trouble making a decision drives the staff bonkers. This type of non-leadership frustrates the hell out of everyone. And it's hard for that boss to hold their respect. The staff will get frustrated having to make multiple U-turns. They need to have confidence that the end result of their efforts will be a decision. Any decision.

Harry ran a large division for years, and while his division was successful, his claim to fame was his inability to make a decision. He was, in fact, legendary for it. He knew it and would laugh about himself. At one company, there would be announcements over the intercom: "Will so and so please come to reception," or "Will so and so please come to the loading dock?" One day, the VP sales that worked for the indecisive person got on the loudspeaker and said, "Will Harry please come to a DECISION?" It got quite a laugh in the building.

Another time, years later, during a staff meeting with around 20 people in a conference room, after various people expressed their opinion on a subject for which we were trying to determine the go forward strategy, the indecisive executive was unusually quiet. The company president called on him and asked for his thoughts. Harry replied "I have an opinion, I just don't know what it is yet." The room froze in silence.

MEMO TO MANAGEMENT

Everyone has their own style, and how you make decisions will, to a great extent, be determined by your particular industry. In cases that involve large sums of R&D cash, large legal issues, etc., prudence is important. In cases where the consequences are manageable or where there is clearly one correct way to go, delaying an action could cost you the opportunity and the respect of staff. As a general rule of thumb, if it goes south, is it reversible and what damage, if any, would have been made? If it's not life and death, don't turn it into Armageddon.

LONELY AT THE TOP

"With all due respect, you've got no fuckin' idea what it's like to be number one, every decision you make affects every other facet of every other fuckin' thing, it's too much to deal with almost. And in the end, you're completely alone with it."

Tony Soprano, *The Sopranos*

Guess that's why you get the big bucks.

I have heard of different ways of going about making decisions. Some firms do it by unanimous decision. One firm gives everyone green and red cards, and they each flash a green for the ideas they like and a red for the ones they don't, and from what I recall, they need all greens. Most companies will get some form of input from department heads, and sometimes, having gone around the table, each department head will sing off the same song sheet. The staff assume that is the way the decision is going to go, but it's not always a democracy. Some leaders, having heard each opinion, may go left even if the group was unanimous in thinking they should go right. I call it a benevolent dictatorship—we get the opinions up front, but it's not necessarily a democracy. There does not have to be a hard and fast rule. It can flip flop between styles.

The important thing is to weigh the pros and cons; what happens if we go, what happens if we don't, what happens if we wait? What will it cost, and what is the potential payoff or loss?

MEMO TO MANAGEMENT

Sometimes you get so stuck in "what we are" that you ensure a no-growth mode. What if Coca Cola or Pepsi viewed themselves as strictly a soda maker? They would not be participating in the growth of bottled water and other categories, such as snacks. When I worked at one company that was famous for the raw material used in their product, they took it to the extreme and would ONLY use it on all products, even if that material was a poor choice for that product, and even if they tried it that way before and failed. That was THEIR material, and come hell or high water, it was going to be used on everything. When I changed that, the unanimous opinion around the table was that I was nuts. It took some time, but eventually they came around and saw us as a design company, not a raw material company. It helped that the first new venture was a success.

YOU'LL GET YOURS AS SOON AS I GET MINE

"Business bad? Fuck you, pay me. Oh, you had a fire? Fuck you, pay me. Place got hit by lightning? Fuck you, pay me."

Paulie Cicero, *Goodfellas*

Got to give Paulie credit for making it pretty clear where he stands on this issue.

When suppliers stop shipping to retailers whose credit rating is so poor they fear they will not get paid, or if they are using a factor to insure the receivables, and the cost of coverage gets so high, the margins shrink to undesirable levels, the retailer's shelves get barren pretty quickly, and the cycle intensifies into a downward spiral.

If companies are slow paying their suppliers, they may eventually get cut off completely. They will not get competitive quotes on new product if the suppliers fear for the safety of the business. Suppliers will not work on low margins on risky business. They will want to make a full margin on whatever business they do get paid on to partially offset whatever business may go unpaid.

When a customer needs a rush order, the one who pays on time will get that preferential treatment, while the offending late payer may be told to go to the end of the line.

Businesses that pay in full and on time are far more likely to get suppliers to invest in tooling, R&D, and other efforts to make things work. Those that don't get less cooperation, reducing their chance of survival.

Whatever industry you are in, word gets around. If you think your troubles or practices will be kept secret, you are wrong.

MEMO TO MANAGEMENT

Focus on payment terms. It makes so much sense, but many companies are oblivious to it. Some suppliers charge when the product ships. Other suppliers may give you 30 or more days to pay. If you are paying your suppliers 30 days from shipment, and it takes 30 days for that shipment to get to your warehouse, payment is due as soon as the goods arrive to your warehouse. It sits there for some time before it ships to your customer. Depending on your customer's payment terms with you, you may not get paid for another 60 days. In this case, if you pay your suppliers on time, you may wind up paying for your goods 90 days or more before you get paid. If you can flip the payment terms to your advantage, it clearly helps your cash flow. Make cash flow a critical issue. I am not sure why it isn't a bigger priority for some firms.

ENOUGH ALREADY WITH THE TEXTS

"Anything I wanted was a phone call away."

Henry Hill, *Goodfellas*

Most, but not all, salespeople know it is easier to be turned down when you are communicating electronically versus actually talking to a person. And some of them know it's easier to be turned down speaking over the phone than actually sitting face to face across from a real live person.

And some purchasing people know that it is more likely that your request for improved pricing is going to be turned down when you make the request electronically versus over the phone, and perhaps a handful realize that your odds will improve again if you get off your behind and go see the supplier and sit across from a real live person to make your case.

Too much reliance is placed on the easy email. And too often, when the CEO inquires how a project is progressing, he or she is told, "Well, I have sent a few emails, and I'm waiting for a response." It's easy to ignore you when I don't actually have to see or speak with you, and it's easy to just type "no" and hit send.

MEMO TO MANAGEMENT

If it's important, show that it's important enough to make the effort to go and speak directly to the other party. Your odds of success go way up. Plus, as a salesperson in a clothing store once told me, "If I can't sell a suit, I'll try and sell a tie." So if your top priority gets turned down during your face to face, perhaps during the conversation, you can gently probe for another opportunity. It may even be an opportunity you were not aware was there for the taking when you initially set out on your mission.

PLUNDER THY NEIGHBOR

"You can't whack a made man on somebody else's crew. There are rules. You never break the rules, capiche?"

Neil Dellacroce, *Gotti*

You are running your department or division and feel all is going well and you are in a good place with your staff. You have open, honest dialogue, you feel you are respected and maybe even liked by some, and all seems good with your world.

Monday morning after the staff meeting, one of your charges asks to speak with you. "What's up?" you ask. He tells you how much he likes working with you and appreciates all that you have done, but he is interested in advancing and trying some new projects, and the head of another department offered him a job. He went to HR and accepted the job, and he starts there in two weeks and wants to make sure all open projects are handled smoothly.

After the person leaves your office, do you call the head of the other department and ask why they didn't come see you first for permission? Did they need to? Do you feel blindsided? Are you now going to scour that person's department every time you have some personnel need to see if there are suitable candidates for you to poach? Do you punch out the other department head when passing him in the hall?

MEMO TO MANAGEMENT

I worked at a company that had a hands-off policy on this subject, meaning there was no policy. They stayed out of it, and it was a free for all. If division leaders felt there was a fit and the employee wanted to move, they moved. It was not ideal and created resentment between division leaders and plenty of gossip amongst the ranks as to what deals they were able to negotiate, playing one division off the other. There should always be a policy on how this sort of thing gets handled. However you decide to handle it is up to you, but make some sort of policy so at least there are rules instead of chaos.

IT'S FUNNY TO SOME PEOPLE
SOME OF THE TIME

"You mean, let me understand this 'cause, ya know, maybe it's me, I'm a little fucked up maybe, but I'm funny how? I mean, funny like I'm a clown? I amuse you? I make you laugh? I'm here to fuckin' amuse you? What do you mean funny, funny how? How am I funny?"

Tommy Devito, *Goodfellas*

A sense of humor is a wonderful tool for anyone, especially a leader in an organization. It loosens people up, gets them to relax around you, and makes work more fun—all good things. Everyone should encourage making the work place a fun place to be and a place you actually look forward to going to.

There is a but, however.

Everyone thinks they are funny, and also smart and good looking. If this were true, there would be no boring people or ugly people or stupid people, so some of us are clearly delusional. Not you or me, of course, but some of those other people.

When handled correctly, using humor is a great tool for positive results., However, it is a disaster when done incorrectly, and you can turn people against you quickly and permanently. So proceed with caution.

MEMO TO MANAGEMENT

If you are going to poke fun at people as a form of humor, best to do the poking at yourself. People will see that you don't take yourself too seriously. You as the person in power run a great risk of offending anyone you are making fun of in your attempt to be funny, particularly if it is in a group session.

MONKEY PROOF

"I want somebody good, and I mean very good, to plant that gun. I don't want my brother coming out of that bathroom with just his dick in his hand."

Sonny Corleone, *The Godfather*

Sales presentations should be called sales preparation. I am a big believer in the upfront work that determines the odds of success in sales. There was a time when I was a retail buyer and people would attempt to sell me their product. It was easily and quickly determined they had not been in one of my stores for a long time. They had no idea what was on my selling floor or what they were competing against.

Sales, marketing, and product development need to work together to review their customer's product assortment; their weak spots, strengths, gaps, price points, and presentation. You need to have a clue as to what you can bring to the table to enhance their assortment. Do the upfront legwork and research. Don't waste your customer's time.

By the same token, don't bury your customer in paperwork—they hate that. Be as brief as you can while making your case. Better yet, try and find out in advance what products the customer really wants to see, or where the opportunities lie. The presentation that addresses "just what I'm looking for" is the way to go; you just need to do some research.

I prefer a sales presentation that is clear and contains the information to explain why our product or service addresses your needs. If done properly, most people can make the presentation by following the script. I also believe in running through these presentations with sales in advance and playing the role of the customer to prepare for likely questions.

MEMO TO MANAGEMENT

A sales planning calendar with seasonal customer planning dates distributed throughout the organization ensures proper planning time for each department, so all know when a preliminary presentation needs to be ready, when samples need to available, when final presentation is due, and what the departmental requirements are for each area and when. The times when the presentation is not perfect are often caused by a lack of planning or advance notice to properly prepare.

THE FREDO SYNDROME

"Taken care of me? Mike, you're my kid brother, and you take care of me? Did you ever think of that? Ever once? Send Fredo off to do this, send Fredo off to do that, take care of some little unimportant night club here and there, pick up somebody at the airport. I'm your older brother, Mike, and I was stepped over! It ain't the way I wanted it! I can handle things. I'm smart. Not like everybody says, I'm dumb. I'm smart, and I want respect!"

Fredo, speaking to his younger brother Michael, *The Godfather*

Something for him, on his own. Ego, resentment, family, all intertwined.

There is a long list of companies started by brilliant, driven individuals who promote their offspring in a planned succession of leadership. Does it always work? Hardly. If you are an employee or executive in a company where Fredo is taking over, and you know of Fredo's shortcomings compared to your own and others' experience and ability, what can you do? Nothing, really. You can be bitter and complain, suck it up, or go work somewhere else. Just don't be under any false illusions that since you are so much smarter than Fredo and so much more qualified for the top spot, you will rightly ascend to the spot. You won't.

People are not fooled if you are not qualified. I knew a company president who embellished his education profile on LinkedIn by omitting the actual college he attended under the education section, replacing it with the prestigious Wharton School, even though his exposure to Wharton was limited to a short-term seminar.

MEMO TO MANAGEMENT

If you work for a Fredo and don't respect him but want to keep your job, you need to at least pretend you respect him. Fredo went against the family because he felt a lack of respect. If your lack of respect is transparent to Fredo, he will go against you, as well. If you cannot bring yourself to this level of being disingenuous, go look for another job.

CHECK IT AND CHECK IT AGAIN

"I hope you don't mind the way I keep going over this Barzini business, it's an old habit. I've spent my whole life trying not to be careless."

Don Corleone, *The Godfather*

You should complete your presentations at least several days before they are due to be distributed. It gives you time to review. Once the data is on the paper, you own it. An infuriating aspect of using PowerPoint is when people read the slide line for line, like the audience is brain-dead. It's even worse if the PowerPoint was sent to the group in advance of the meeting, assuming your colleagues actually read it, which many don't even bother to do.

Take your time to review your presentation, obviously for errors of fact, grammar, and spelling. Also make sure you connect the dots throughout the presentation. There will always be someone in the audience who will relish pointing out that what you state on page 23 does not exactly jive with what is on page

37. Keep the information per slide to a reasonable minimum— no eye chart or crazy, complicated graphs that need a scientist to decipher. Each slide should have a pertinent point to make; otherwise, why is it in there? Make sure you take a slash and burn approach to any page that seems to be going on forever or is too verbose. Keep it as short as possible, each point made in as few words as possible and as few bullets as possible. And don't be repetitive.

MEMO TO MANAGEMENT

The most important fact is that you actually understand and can explain what the data means. If you answer too many questions with, "I'll have to find out and get back to you on that," you did not adequately prepare. Know what the numbers mean. Know what the causes are. Make sure you have formulated an action plan and know the timing it will begin. State when we can expect to see results. State what those results might be and the who, what, and where of the details. Anticipate all questions and have the data handy to deal with them. But if you read a slide, and it automatically makes you think of a question, then that slide should include information to address the obvious question the slide will cause. Head that baby off at the pass.

BAD BOSS DAY

"Every once in a while, I'd have to take a beating, but by then, I didn't care. The way I saw it, everyone takes a beating sometime."

Henry Hill, *Goodfellas*

You are comfortable with your boss and consider yourself to be on friendly terms. The strange thing about bosses is, every once in a while, and sometimes out of the blue, they decide to act like the boss. You might think to yourself, what's bugging him today? Who knows? Who cares?

In a sense, every conversation you have with your boss is like a job interview. Every conversation, no matter how small, provides you with an opportunity to have your boss walk away thinking how sharp you are—or what a dumb bag of rocks you are.

If you say something that causes the veins in your boss's neck to bulge, try and change the subject or hide under the desk. With some bosses, you are better off being proactive with information, and with others, you are better off leaving them alone until they seek you out. Either way, you need to figure this out quickly.

I was returning from a three week Asia trip. On my first day back in the office, I thought it would be nice to stop by my boss's office to say hello as a sort of courtesy to let him know I was in the building and to see if he had questions about the trip. He did not say hello, he did not ask how the trip was, or how pleasant my return flight was. He just starting yelling at the top of his lungs that the numbers looked terrible and I had better do something about it. That was the last time I ever went to his office without being summoned.

MEMO TO MANAGEMENT

> If you are the boss giving the beating, don't let the employee stew too long before reaching out to have a more civil conversation. The topic is not important, just touch base in a low-key manner on something. It's your job to make the first move toward reestablishing the relationship. Sort of like never going to bed mad.

DIE ON THE SWORD

"All right, you proved your point. You broke into my vault. Congratulations, you're a dead man."

Terry Benedict, *Oceans Eleven*

If you are arguing with your spouse and you want to break out the Google search to prove that you are right and they are wrong, that is your choice, and may determine where you will be sleeping that night.

Debates with your boss and coworkers are a different story. With your boss, it really gets down to winning the battle and losing the war, perhaps. It depends on the boss and the situation, but for sure you need to pick your spots and your methods.

I find it even touchier with customers. You want to make your case and have them believe you or your facts, but if they become obstinate and basically call your presentation bull spit, how do you prove you are right and they are wrong? Tread lightly, for one thing. It's not like you're arguing with a buddy over a beer in a bar where you can call him a dope. Your best chance of success is taking one of their points and using that to help you make your case. You will be using their point of view as part of the solution.

In the movie, *My Big Fat Greek Wedding*, the women knew they had to get the man to think it was his idea. When they manipulated him into thinking he had solved the problem himself, he was thrilled with himself, and tapped the side of his head saying, "Eh? The man." You need to do the same.

MEMO TO MANAGEMENT

The bigger the group in the meeting, the touchier things get. But by all means, try and avoid actual anger, or at least try and avoid showing it. One of the absolute worst things a boss can do, in my opinion, is to yell at someone in a meeting. Getting yelled at makes the person feel like they are back in grade school, and it is demeaning. On top of that, it's not a fair fight. The person can't yell back at the boss, can they? Never yell. You can make your point in a civilized manner without throwing your weight around.

DOUBLESPEAK

**"Say WHAT again, say WHAT again! I dare you!
I double dare you!"**

Jules Winnfield, *Pulp Fiction*

Okay, so you have a point to make. You feel it is a brilliant idea. You have the pitch perfected. You approach your boss with it. He pisses on it. You, momentarily stunned, regroup and take the battle up again, and again he pisses on it.

What do you do? For me, two strikes does not mean I am out, two strikes means I live to fight another day. I figure going back to your boss a THIRD time might be annoying enough where three strikes may actually mean I am out. So I have a two strikes rule.

Occasionally, if your presentation actually did make sense, your boss may come back to you in a day or two and say it could have merit. Sometimes these ideas just need to simmer like a stew. I had a boss who would bring the same idea up a few days later like it was his idea. I would remind him that we had discussed this a few days earlier. He was a bit like the guy who never admits defeat. He would say my idea was similar, but the way he is approaching it is different. Okay, then. Brilliant idea, boss.

MEMO TO MANAGEMENT

If you are not sure you like an idea, ask questions before killing it. Maybe you don't understand it entirely, or maybe parts of it will work even if other parts won't. And for goodness' sake, if it is a good idea, give recognition to the originator, and in front of others, if possible. Encourage ideas by recognizing them in a positive manner.

MY WAY OR THE HIGHWAY

"Listen to me very carefully, there are three ways of doing things around here, the right way, the wrong way, and the way that I do it. You understand?"

Ace Rothstein, *Casino*

People want your input until they don't want it. Is that clear?

When you are told by your superiors that they want your ideas on how to do things differently, how they admire your past "best practices" approach and have a lot they can learn from your experience, tread lightly.

They will quickly get to the point where they are tired of hearing how they could or should be doing things differently.

One reason is ego. Another is resentment.

The best advice in these cases is to stay in your lane. When you are suggesting improvements that are DIRECTLY under your purview and charges, it's one thing. When you suggest improvements in other areas, people get pissed, even if you are right.

MEMO TO MANAGEMENT

Don't be so touchy about turf, and pay more attention to doing things the right way, ego be damned. I approved a multi-million-dollar program with a major retailer based on written pricing information I received from our overseas office. The overseas office handled all supplier communication. After giving the go ahead to sales and the customer, overseas came back and said they gave me the wrong pricing information, eroding my profit by hundreds of thousands of dollars. When I requested a copy of the written quote from the supplier, the overseas office told me there was none, it was just a phone conversation between the supplier and the merchandiser in the overseas office. This is clearly the wrong way to do things.

When I complained, as this mistake hit my P&L, the head of the overseas office went to the company head and complained about my insistence of getting quotes in writing. They were "too busy" for that. Amazingly enough, the company head agreed with the overseas staff and basically told me to stay in my lane.

INDIVIDUAL PASSION COUNTS
WITHIN TEAMWORK

"A man becomes preeminent; he's expected to have ENTHUSIASM. ENTHUSIASMS, ENTHUSIASMS. What are mine? What draws my admiration? What is that which gives me joy? Baseball! A man stands alone at the plate. This is the time for what? For individual achievement. There he stands alone. But in the field, what? Part of a team. Teamwork. Looks, throws, catches, hustles, part of one big team. Bats himself the live long day, Babe Ruth, Ty Cobb, and so on. If his team don't field, what is he? You follow me? No one, sunny day, the stands are full of fans. What does he have to say? I'm going out there for myself, but I get nowhere unless the team wins."

Al Capone, right before he bashed a guy in the head with a baseball bat, *The Untouchables*

When most people are hiring, they look for people with passion, and for good reason. Education, brains, and hard work all fall short without passion.

People with passion generally do a better job because they take more pride in what they do. They want to do more than just get the job done. They want to excel, and they generally love what they do.

Passionate people sometimes don't work as well in a team environment. If others don't share their level of passion, they get frustrated. So the dynamics of these situations need to be monitored.

The challenge with team projects is making sure something actually gets done. If everyone is too focused on championing their own version of events, things can go in circles. People can spend too much time devoted to their desire to hear themselves talk. A facilitator is often required, hopefully someone who knows what they are doing. In some cases, you may want to have an individual execute the project first, and then present it to the group for feedback. This way you get something accomplished before the group talks it to death. Just make sure the group is not more concerned with tearing it apart than working toward a constructive conclusion.

MEMO TO MANAGEMENT

Individual stars often drive the team to winning streaks versus a collection of mediocre role players. Recognize the stars and give them the leadership role in the team project. The challenge in the team approach is in landing the plane and making a decision. Let someone be the pilot, preferably someone who knows how to fly.

LOST AND FOUND

**"How could we be lost like this?
We're in fucking New Jersey."**

Christopher replies, "We're in SOUTH Jersey."

Paulie Walnuts talking to Christopher, *The Sopranos*

Companies recognize growth can come from one of a few places:
- You can sell more to your existing customers.
- You can sell to new customers in your current channel of distribution.
- You can sell to new customers in new channels of distribution.
- You can sell to new customers in other countries.

Before you go outside your existing channels of distribution, you want to make sure it's not as complicated as going from North Jersey to South Jersey, lest you get lost in the woods.

Have you properly vetted the new channel? Its main customers? Their needs? What it takes to succeed? Do you have adequate knowledge of the cost of entry and the competitors' strengths and weaknesses? Why does the market need you?

MEMO TO MANAGEMENT

It is usually better to be first than it is to be better. Not always, as Apple proved. But you need to either be better, be first, or be different. Otherwise, you might fall into a "price only" proposition, which is a loser's game. A few lucky companies have a brand that is so powerful that it saves the day, no matter what you do, but those are fewer and fewer. If you can manage to have a series of first-to-market opportunities, you position yourself for prolonged success. Look for seams in the market. Don't fall into the common trap of over-reliance on line extensions. Customers play the add one, drop one game, and your company treads water.

CREATIVITY LIVES HERE

"The only thing I found in the street was my first wife."

Eugene Pontcorvo, *The Sopranos*

Where do you send your product development team? Looking at trade shows in your own industry is often boring, and they just show what already exists. They work great if your goal is to be the second or third company introducing the item.

There is a benefit to looking in the street. How are people using their products, what are they struggling with, what needs do you see? How can you take what exists and differentiate it to the point that it feels new and improved?

Steve Jobs said, "A lot of times people don't know what they want until you show it to them."

Henry Ford said, "If I had asked people what they wanted, they would have said faster horses."

Thomas Edison said, "Opportunity is missed by most people because it is dressed in overalls and looks like work."

In the history of product development, those three are in the Hall of Fame.

I rate product development in these tiers:

At the base of the ladder, I put line extensions.

A step up, I put new categories or subcategories of product.

At the top, I put first-to-market opportunities.

Figure out a way to do something, even if it has actually been done before, so you can say, "This is the first time anyone has done this product this way."

MEMO TO MANAGEMENT

Institute a 3 and 3 product development plan: Three years of a rolling development plan combined with the three-tier product development level outlined above.

Force your staff to rank their ideas according to the three-tier structure. It will force them to acknowledge if they are living too much on the ground floor of line extensions or truly seeking to create something new.

Challenge staff for out of the box thinking. Buyers and consumers react to something new, otherwise they are not motivated to buy a slightly rehashed version of something they already have.

Be better, be first, be different. Or be gone.

DRONE ON, AND ON, AND ON

"No more advice on how to patch things up, just help me win, please, alright?"

Sonny Corleone, *The Godfather*

Meetings can suck the life out of your day and accomplish little if you let the drones drone on till heads drop and hit the table.

If you want to establish rules for meetings, as some do, that is your call. I've seen or heard of limiting time for each person to speak, running a tight agenda for the meeting that MUST be followed, limiting the meeting time to a strict limit, and all sorts of other things. Whatever you do, if the meeting is not productive, you will not be the only person aware of it. Everyone in the room will know it and wonder why in the world you don't do something about it.

Sonny's quote holds a key to solving the issue. Too many people make speeches, or go on rants, and at some point, you lose sight of what the question was or what the issue was we were trying to solve in the first place.

MEMO TO MANAGEMENT

If you have a person that is more intent on hearing their own soliloquy as if preparing for their opening on Broadway, you need to pull the person back to reality. Invoke Sonny's quote, something to this effect: "That is a wonderful thought, and when we have more time, we would all love to hear it in further detail. But right now, we have a specific issue that we need to address. I'd like the comments to focus on that issue and what we can actually do right now to win in this particular instance." If that does not work, ask the person to leave the meeting.

WALKING DEAD MAN

**"It's a Sicilian message. It means
Luca Brazzi sleeps with the fishes."**

Tessio, *The Godfather*

You usually know you're on the way out before they actually
tell you that you are sleeping with the fishes. At least you know
you're getting closer to the water.

What signs to look for and what to do about it could determine how quickly you rebound or possibly beat the rap.

If the company is performing poorly, about to merge with
another company, or up for sale, these are all obvious times to
refresh your resume. But aside from these circumstances, look
for the subtle changes.

Your gut will tell you something is amiss in many cases. Does
your boss seem to avoid you more than usual? Does he seem
short with you? Has his eye contact changed? Does he communicate more often with your direct reports without looping you

in as much? Is your opinion sought out less or discarded more readily? Are you not on group emails that you were usually on? Do you feel you are being picked on or singled out for criticism more than usual?

MEMO TO MANAGEMENT

Be proactive if any of these warning signs flash. Update your resume at once, and make sure your networking skills are sharpened. Make sure you are listed on pertinent job sites as available. And reach out to any close and trusted industry sources to let them know to keep you in mind if something comes up. It's easier to find a job before you actually need a job. And at your current job, don't forget that it is still your current job, and by that, I mean, don't hide. Don't do anything to hasten your exit or antagonize anyone. Be professional, work as hard as ever, and hope for the best. If they do let you go, go out with your head up and avoid trashing your former employer or boss.

WHEN THE GOING GETS TOUGH, THE TOUGH DO LESS

"Sonny is thinking of going to the mattresses."

Clemenza, *The Godfather*

As we entered the Great Recession of 2008-2009, the mood at the board meeting was somber. A member of the board said, "If you can survive this year and stay in business, it will be an accomplishment."

Well, that is not exactly like Knute Rockne telling the boys to "win one for the Gipper," but we got the message that we were in for a bumpy ride.

We realized that some of the grand plans we had to build the company should be put on hold. We focused on the very core of our business: products in core categories. We continued to introduce new products while competitors were pulling back, but we did it in a focused, controlled manner, and only on items and categories we had an extra comfort level and confidence for. If it was slightly risky, we delayed it. If it had a longer than 12-month payback, we delayed it. When customers came to us for price cuts due to the economic climate, we said no. We held firm, not doing anything to reduce our own margins. All raises and new hires were put on hold. Travel was cut to a minimum unless absolutely needed. If we could get suppliers to come to us instead of us going to them to save money, we did so. Anything resembling upper class travel or accommodation was cut to coach level. Anything that was "nice to have" was cut, and only those things that were "had to have" were kept.

While we watched our expenses and did not cut a single selling price, we did go to all of our suppliers with a vengeance. And not just for the product suppliers, but for every service imaginable. We made sure we exaggerated our situation as worse than it actually was. Our suppliers wanted to do what they could to help us survive rather than have a loyal client go out of business.

MEMO TO MANAGEMENT

We finished that year with the best results in over a decade. If you do the things we did in tough times, perhaps you should be looking at how you do business in good times. Maybe some of these methods can or should carry over to normal times. Don't get fat and lazy in good times.

PERSONALLY SPEAKING, IF IT'S MY BUSINESS, IT'S QUITE PERSONAL

"It's not personal, Sonny, it's business."

Michael Corleone, *The Godfather*

In the movie, *You've Got Mail*, Kathleen Kelly, the character played by Meg Ryan, is confronted with this quote from *The Godfather*. She replied, "What is that supposed to mean? I am so sick of that. All that means is that wasn't personal to you. But it was personal to me. It's "personal" to a lot of people. And what's so wrong with being personal, anyway?"

So, call me a fence straddler because I think they are both right. It is personal and it isn't personal. You say hello, I say goodbye. It's like saying, "I saw the guy get hit by that train, but I didn't feel a thing."

When you are the person making the tough personnel decisions, you have to be detached. There is no way around it. But the person being terminated probably agrees with Kathleen

Kelly. And if you are not empathetic or too cavalier in how you deal with these things, you will certainly offend the person unnecessarily.

But if you come across as too caring and take too long to tell the person they are fired, you are basically prolonging the torture. Best to be quick and understanding. Try to sound as sympathetic as possible. In most cases, the person just wants to get out of there as quickly as possible.

MEMO TO MANAGEMENT

There are two sides to this coin, and at the risk of sounding contradictory, here goes. You should always avoid rushing to judgment. The decision to fire anyone is not to be taken lightly, and you must realize that it has severe consequences to that person and their family. So do what you can to turn the situation around. The other side of the coin? Usually you know if a person is lacking ,and when you do pull the trigger, you often tell yourself you should have done it sooner.

YOU GET WHAT YOU NEGOTIATE

"You see, life's a negotiation, it's all give and take."

Jimmy Hoffa, *Hoffa*

Your margin is more often than not determined by your first cost: the actual cost to buy or make that product. This is often more important than what you wholesale it for. Why? Because sometimes you don't have full control over the retail price point, particularly if the market expects to see that item at a certain retail. In these cases, your selling price is determined by the market's expectation of what they should pay for that item.

An intelligent approach to purchasing your products can have a dramatic impact on your bottom line, perhaps as much as any other single action.

Some common mistakes that are often made include:

- No insistence on a set number of multiple bids.
- No insistence on written DETAILED quotes.

- No documentation of monetary exchange rates or raw material costs at the time of the quote. Attempt to get a downward adjustment if either turn in your favor at some point in the future.
- No understanding of the BOM (Bill of Material process) in price quotations.
- No understanding of the importance of building out a menu pricing chart for your products.
- No detailed databank of suppliers that could be cross-referenced across divisions.
- Asking for things in the wrong manner from a legal, practical, and cost perspective.
- Not knowing what parts the supplier actually made versus outsourced.
- Not knowing what components had the largest impact on the product's MOQ (Minimum Order Quantity).
- Not knowing the cost impact of every design and engineering change before it was implemented.

I could go on and on with this subject.

MEMO TO MANAGEMENT

> The cost you pay is as significant a driver to your bottom line as any other single event in your company.

The best example I have seen of this is IKEA, and no one in my experience has come close. They fully understood and utilized the BOM review process. If they wanted to buy 5 million lamps, instead of going to the lamp supplier and asking for a quote on that complete item, they would have cost engineers develop the BOM. They would review which component was manufactured versus outsourced at each potential supplier. Then they would actually go to the component parts suppliers that the lamp supplier would use. Many "manufacturers" are mainly assembly lines of outsourced product with one or two components manufactured in-house. Goodness, look at the automobile business. "Made in America" is often supplemented with imported parts.

Anyway, IKEA would visit each of the lamps' parts suppliers. For instance, if they were buying 5 million of that particular lamp, and they carried 100 lamps in their assortment, they would go to every supplier of cords, shades, switches, harps, all the parts that go into every lamp. Most lamp "manufacturers" manufacture a small portion of the item and outsource the majority. IKEA would tell each of these suppliers to quote on their entire business. They would offer the manufacturers the hope that they could secure an annual order of 500 Million pieces (5 million time 100 SKUs). I am, of course, estimating the numbers, but believe me, they are huge.

Why don't more companies operate this way? Because many don't understand the process or the value of BOM cost engineering. They just flop around asking suppliers for their best price instead of going to the supplier and saying, "Look, this is what this part should cost you, and here are my approved suppliers for each of the components you are going to outsource, and here are the costs for each of those outsourced parts, and I'll give you xx % for assembly, profit and overhead. So here is what I need, can you handle my business at this price for 5 million pieces?"

Do you have cost engineers on staff? Maybe you should.

INVISIBLE PERSON

"A real grievance can be resolved, differences can be resolved, but an imaginary hurt, a slight, that mother-fucker gonna hate you till the day he dies."

Jimmy Hoffa, *Hoffa*

Everyone that attends a meeting with a supplier, a customer, or any business contact usually knows the cast of characters and their rank or importance to the other side. Or at least they should.

While is it customary to place the majority of your focus, eye contact, and efforts on the decision maker of the group, there is a limit to how slanted this effort should be.

If you ignore the lowest ranking members of the meeting, you might come across as a pompous big shot who feels they don't even deserve your acknowledgment. Aside from bad manners, it could come back to work against you as they rise through the ranks and take on a more prominent position within their own organization or go to another company and assume a position of authority.

No one likes to be disregarded or made to feel small and unimportant.

MEMO TO MANAGEMENT

Go out of your way to address each member of the meeting at the outset. Make sure at the conclusion of the meeting to thank each person for their time and participation. Too often, I have seen a meeting conclude, and the top attendee from one side only shakes hands with and thanks the top attendee from the other side, basically ignoring the fact that there were other attendees. A top executive can create goodwill by personally thanking a low-level attendee for being there, and a quick "nice to meet you" goes a long way toward how that person thinks of the executive. If they ever meet up again on more equal terms, most people will remember how they were treated.

HOLD THE HAMMER

"I won't pay, I know too much about extortion."

Tony Soprano, *The Sopranos*

It's good to have strong relationships with your suppliers. Always strive for developing good, solid, long-term relationships.

There is a BUT, however.

The BUT exists when the comfort level gets a bit too comfortable. Especially dealing with suppliers in Asia.

This happens if you develop such a strong supplier relationship that you basically know where a certain project will wind up before the bids are in. Or if you stop actively seeking multiple bids because, in your mind, the supplier is already chosen. If these thoughts are in your mind, the supplier probably has this figured out, as well. In this case, the odds of ever getting the best cost are slim.

If the supplier knows you are in a rush and must make a decision and start today, odds are you are not getting the best price. If your schedule is known, and they know you are not seeing other suppliers, odds are you are not getting the best price. If you are leaving for home and still have open projects, and you tell them it MUST be decided before you leave, you are probably not getting the best price. Time often works against you.

MEMO TO MANAGEMENT

You must have viable sourcing options, or you are not holding the hammer. Once the supplier is holding the hammer, you are not going to win. Try and get detailed quotes from multiple suppliers before you begin the series of supplier meetings. Otherwise, you won't have enough market intelligence to sufficiently converse in your early meetings. Also, armed with this data, you know the starting point and can work from there during your trip. You must have at least two or three significant and active suppliers for each category, if possible. How you split the business is up to you, but preferably so each person has enough business from you to remain important.

ARE WE DOWNSIZING AGAIN?

"You are going to can a lot of people. Make sure you do it the first day. That way, the ones that are left don't feel insecure, ya see, what they feel is grateful. You do it piecemeal and they are going to turn against you."

Jimmy Hoffa

Eventually staff cuts will need to be made, sometimes severe, deep cuts. Sometimes these cuts are a result of business downturn and sometimes they're due to mergers or other corporate restructuring. People get it and are more okay with it than you probably think.

They are okay with it as long as you don't keep doing it over and over again. That gets old quickly. People spend some of their time complaining about it and much of their time looking for another job once this slash and burn merry-go-round gets in motion. Your morale goes to hell, your staff starts jumping ship, and the result is ugly.

Handle it so the cuts are on the same day. Follow this with a company or departmental meeting explaining why the cuts were made and that the remaining people are safe. And we are going to battle with this group. We have a game plan on how we are going to be successful. No one needs to be concerned, everyone can relax and focus on their job, and their efforts are greatly appreciated.

MEMO TO MANAGEMENT

Communication is critical, but not as critical as making sure it is true. You can't come out and say we are done with cuts, everyone relax, and then start slashing again in a month. Perhaps when you reassure them, you leave yourself a slight out, such as: "No one can predict the future, but we fully expect that this is it." This way, if something unforeseen happens, you technically did not lie, but for practical purposes, you're as close to certain as possible that the cuts are complete when you make your announcement.

BOMBS AWAY, BUT WE'RE OK

"I know some of you come from upstate, Connecticut and Jersey. I won't keep you long. Nobody knows who killed them, so don't ask, no one has to look over their shoulder here. You're the Gambino family and don't you ever believe anyone anywhere, is going to fuck with us. Now go home, and drive carefully because, believe me, that's the most dangerous part of your lives. Thank you for being here."

John Gotti, as he called his entire staff together right after two employees were blown up in their car, *Gotti*

Any bad news, whether it be layoffs, shutdowns, or the loss of a major customer that will severely impact the business, causes employee concern and gossip. People become more concerned with "Are we going to be okay?" than doing their job as they are having trouble concentrating and thinking straight.

It's your job to set them straight and get them back in the game.

After bad news, you don't want a pep rally approach—you need to acknowledge the seriousness of the situation. But you also need to strike a calm and positive approach and offer reassurance that everything will be okay. We have your back.

The fact that Gotti immediately addressed the issue and did it with his full staff assembled shows good leadership. I am not sure how many of those in attendance were calm enough to drive their own cars home versus taking public transportation, but Gotti's intentions were good.

MEMO TO MANAGEMENT

Whether you are speaking to your employees or directly to the consumer, the faster you address a problem and offer reassurance, the better. If the problem is self-inflicted, you need to 'fess up' and say you will do better; here is how we are going to go about it. You are allowed to screw up, providing you acknowledge it. Apologize for it and offer a clear game plan and timetable for making it right.

BELL CURVE

"It's good to be in on something from the ground floor. I came in too late for that, and I know. But lately, I'm getting the feeling that I came in at the end, the best is over."

Tony Soprano, *The Sopranos*

Product life cycles can't be ignored. Like Branch Rickey, the general manager of the Brooklyn Dodgers in the 1940s, said, "Trade a player a year too early rather than a year too late." You should keep track of the product's life cycle on the bell curve and consider killing it yourself, providing you have the planned replacement in development.

By moving on your own product early, you can avoid the next phase of the slowdown, thereby avoiding continued declining sales. You can also anticipate your customers' inevitable request for markdown money or product returns once the item is officially designated as a dropped item. Let it die a natural death in a quiet, unannounced manner. When your warehouse inventory as well as the customers' inventory is low, make your move and kill it. Your cost to mark it down will be at the low point if you time it right.

Remember to train your sales staff on timing and announcements so all customers, or at least the ones you want to protect, are handled properly and communication does not lag or aggravate people. Make sure any pending promos are covered and you review any potential customer issues before finalizing the dates to discontinue and replace.

MEMO TO MANAGEMENT

Make sure to do a few things correctly in this plan. Make sure your accounts put in the replacement SKU so you don't wind up losing shelf space. You want to drop the SKU you want to drop and add the SKU you want to add WHEN you are ready to ship and when the former item's inventory is at its low point.

DOES THAT HURT?

"Alright, so he got shot in the foot, why is it such a big fuckin' deal?"

Tommy Devito, *Goodfellas*

In the prior section, we talked about product life cycle management and how to control the demise of one product and the roll-out of another.

If you are seeking a direct replacement of an existing item, the new product is most likely a newer version of the one it's replacing rather than an entirely new direction—a refresh, if you will, to keep the item sales from flatlining. And while the timing of shipping the new SKU is critical to avoid stock-outs and loss of sales, you need to avoid shooting yourself in the foot.

MEMO TO MANAGEMENT

As in the case of general line extensions, the direct "SKU for SKU" replacement needs to have management of the margin—are you switching out a SKU at a higher margin for a SKU with a lower margin? If so, go back to the drawing board, unless you are being delusional with the "we will make up for it in volume" rap. Margin maintenance, or better yet, margin enhancement covers all sorts of sins. If you are making tight margin going in, you are going to be coming out in a pair of skinny jeans that don't look good on you.

CAREER CHOICES ARE NOT A MYSTERY

"This is the price you pay for the life you chose."

Michael Corleone, *The Godfather*

I've heard all sorts of people in all sorts of jobs complain about aspects of their job, from the hours, the pay, the travel, etc.; all were part of the deal going in.

Teachers ARE underpaid, but they knew the pay scale before choosing to become a teacher.

Likewise, police and firemen have dangerous jobs. If that bothers you after you've chosen that profession, I have to ask, what were you thinking?

If money is your main priority, choose a profession that pays well. Seems obvious and simple enough, doesn't it?

If your goal is to help people, maybe the medical profession is your calling.

Your choices have consequences; make sure you choose wisely.

MEMO TO MANAGEMENT

Traveling businessmen and women often complain about the travel. Several people at different jobs complained so much, I made the same offer to all of them, at different times and at different companies.

It went something like this: I will eliminate all your travel. Every day, from now on, you will work in this office, and I will figure out how to have someone else cover your travel needs. You can keep your title and salary; you will just never travel again. I'll assign that task to another individual or I'll do it myself. The answer every time was the same. NO ONE ever accepted that deal, and NO ONE ever again complained about traveling, not even once.

SMELL TEST

"The night of the fight, you might feel a slight sting. That's pride fucking with you."

Marcellus Wallace, *Pulp Fiction*

If the milk smells bad, throw it out. Don't risk getting sick over the cost of a gallon of milk.

If something does not feel right, you know it. Ask yourself if it passes the smell test. Smell bad to you? Then you know you are going down a path you should not be going down.

For instance, the smell test can be applied to a product launch. Maybe you are not comfortable that all the engineering has been worked out and you are rushing to launch before you are sold that the kinks have been worked out. When Optimum Cable first launched and nationally advertised their Altice One as a great new product, it appeared they launched with too many programming bugs. At that time, their service calls for this product went through the roof. SOMEONE at that company had to know that the timing of that product launch was not passing the smell test.

Or maybe you chose a supplier who is not perfect, and you know it, but no one else is stepping up. You figure any supplier is better than no supplier, even if the supplier is not the best. When the shipment is late or the quality subpar, remember that smell that you sensed before the program was awarded.

MEMO TO MANAGEMENT

Hold firm to the smell test for one of the most valuable aspects of your business—your BRAND. What if you sense you are adding a product, a line extension, or a new category to your brand that does not perfectly represent what your brand stands for, but you proceed and pinch your nostrils because you want the expected extra sales? You should have taken a deep breath and gotten a nose full of common sense. The potential damage to the brand is not worth it if the new venture does not pass the smell test for your brand.

TALK TALK TALK

"In fact, the expiration date was last week on all your bullshit with that."

Tony Soprano, *The Sopranos*

So, you have a plan for turning around your business, for driving sales and improving margins.

You are meticulous in outlining the problem and what needs to be done.

You are cutting the low margin SKUs or categories to focus on higher margin core businesses.

You are adding new products that should truly produce INCREMENTAL sales.

You are properly valuing your dead inventory.

You are focusing on excellent design and outstanding quality backed by solid engineering and solid testing.

You are doing such a good job and are getting such good feedback that, in your quarterly review, you proclaim that you expect to see positive results by next quarter.

Next quarter comes and one of the main suppliers had an issue, and the roll-out is delayed.

The quarter after that, the main customer has a top-down edict from senior management that, due to poor sales, they will not be adding any new programs this season because of inventory issues.

So now you go to two MORE quarterly reviews still promising the turnaround, after all these issues were unexpected.

MEMO TO MANAGEMENT

> If you participate in a few consecutive quarterly reviews or board meetings with the same song lyrics, with the same lack of results, you can expect someone to treat you with a version of the Tony Soprano quote above. What you can do is temper the expected date of the turnaround. Don't get over your skis. Undersell until you actually deliver.

A GUT FEELING OF DATA

"Fear knocked at the door, faith answered, there was no one there."

Christopher, *The Sopranos*

You know your new product is going to be great, you just know it.

You have that feeling in your gut that it is really going to be a strong seller.

You have faith in your conviction.

Maybe you could use some data to go with that conviction.

Make sure someone is behind the door when you knock.

Have you ever had others express doubts about something you were doing but you were so in love with the idea that you plowed ahead anyway? Did it work out okay?

Most products don't work as well as people hope, sort of like the success rate of new restaurants. But your batting average needs to be that the cost of failure is more than covered by your successes.

Steve Jobs once said, "People don't know what they want until you show it to them. That's why I never rely on market research. Our task is to read things that are not yet on the page." Personally, I like to look at a few sources. One is industry data to see what areas or micro-areas are growing, or even better, ABOUT to grow. I like to compile the likes and dislikes available via consumer reviews to make sure we are not adding features that people are already telling us they don't like. And I like to evaluate trend forecasting in general for design, lifestyle changes, and demographic shifts. You need to put all of these into your mental blender and see what comes out. Trends, plus consumer reviews, plus data, equals a decent shot at success.

MEMO TO MANAGEMENT

If you are going to fail, make sure it is not a BIG fail. Small fails can be quickly overcome and are often overlooked. Big fails get people fired. Start slow till you know for sure. You can make a career out of a single big winner. You can also kill a career from a single big failure. Fail small.

SWOT THIS

"I don't feel like I need to wipe everybody out, just my enemies."

Michael Corleone, *The Godfather*

This is a bit of Sun Tzu from Michael.

Most companies prepare or should prepare a SWOT analysis on themselves and their main competitors: Strengths, Weakness, Opportunities and Threats. It is good to revisit and refresh these on an annual basis.

MEMO TO MANAGEMENT

When looking at your competitors (enemies), the key component of this exercise is to look for the weakness in their strength. You read that correctly. Then figure out how to flank that strength. If their strength is in their easy-to-assemble product, is there an opportunity for a fully assembled product at the same price? If their strength is in their durability, is there an opportunity for a cheaper disposable version? If their strength is in their easy to clean feature, is it possible to offer a self-cleaning option? If their strength is their established brand, there could be an opportunity for a radical disrupter brand that has more youth appeal.

PARALYZED OR PRESENTING?

"They're going to be scared shit of you, believe me, so don't worry about nothin."

Clemenza, *The Godfather*

In various polls, people have listed making presentations to a group as one of the most terrifying things they have to face. Shame, because making presentations effectively is one of the best ways to climb the corporate ladder.

When else do you get the chance for a large group, which often includes your superiors whom you rarely get the opportunity to even speak with, to see how wonderful you are? These moments are the best opportunities you will likely ever get to impress people several levels above you. Relish the opportunity and prepare like hell.

It helps to have a good personality. It helps not to be boring. But it is horrible to make forced jokes that don't work, so unless you are really funny, skip that part and just be professional.

If humor works for you, that is great, just don't try and force it. Some people can do presentations off the cuff, others have to practice and memorize and read from notes. I find that those who read from detailed, long-winded notes are the worst. If you must use notes, try and use bullets that feature a word or two (at most) that remind you of the topic to speak to. You should already know the details, so these flash card reminders should just be refreshers to jog your memory. If you are using a screen, a word or phrase on each slide in the presentation should serve as your notes to jog your memory. Just don't read the slide, for goodness' sake.

MEMO TO MANAGEMENT

Help your younger staff members ease into presentations by giving them easy bit parts that are quick and painless. Once they have made a few cameo appearances in your presentation, they will see that they were not eaten alive, and their fear will subside. Also, if you are more comfortable with a podium, use it, but move around and talk, rather than clinging to the podium with a death grip. One effective method is to engage the audience. This puts them a bit on notice, and gives you power that they don't have; after all, you are the one with the microphone. Don't abuse anyone (unless you have to), but by calling on a specific person, mentioning their name, and asking a question, you will certainly get everyone's attention. If they were starting to doze off, or checking their email, they will snap to attention. They will think, holy moly, I didn't know he was going to be calling us out, I'd better pay attention. Damn right.

Plus, engaging the audience gives you a breather and avoids the long speech-type presentation that gets boring quickly. The active back and forth is more enjoyable and often leads to something constructive.

Personally, I never thought that picturing your audience naked was a good idea; scary maybe, but not good.

CLOSE TO THE VEST

"Never tell anyone outside the family what you're thinking again."

Don Corleone, *The Godfather*

The family is, of course, the company. Outside the family includes your competitors, your customers, your suppliers, and various industry sources such as trade papers and service providers you hire for various consulting or out-sourced work.

What you always have to remember is most of these people deal with everyone in your industry. Your supplier probably supplies all your competitors, or many of them. The industry trade paper covers the entire industry. Your customers deal with every single supplier in the industry. The person you hire as outsourced talent to help with videos, marketing, packaging, sourcing, etc. does the same for dozens, if not hundreds, of clients. If you think what you say to them is as secure as confessing to your priest, you are nuts. Some of them are totally reliable, some are not.

As important as what you say or don't say is when you say it. I mentioned earlier about timing of announcements in trade stories. I worked for a large company where I ran my divisions, but marketing was a corporate function that was independent of the divisions. They would arrange trade paper interviews and were always anxious to release news or exciting new products. They would sometimes arrange full page ads as well as interviews featuring these products. Great, except sometimes these ads ran six months before the product was ready to ship. Or to put it another way, about as long as it would take a competitor to develop their own version and be on the market was about the time we were shipping. Not a brilliant strategy, if you ask me.

At this same company, a president of a different division was talking to a trade paper about a new program his area was rolling out. When asked about his targeted customers and channels of distribution, he mentioned that he thought it had good potential in the "off price" channel. These are all fine stores, but when you are rolling out a new program and hope to sell it to "full price" retailers, best not to advertise that you intend at the outset to also supply the very retailers that are bound to undercut the full price retailers. Not smart.

MEMO TO MANAGEMENT

I think it wise to train or instruct anyone who is going to speak to trade papers on the best way to approach these situations. Most companies don't—they just throw the people in the water. Once the article is out there, the damage is done, and it's too late. I also suggest having a policy for who can speak to trade papers; often times you see junior marketing managers getting quoted. I don't think that is wise. Many professional sports teams prohibit the assistant coaches from speaking to the press, and I think some restrictions on who can speak to the press are wise for every company. If you don't have that in your policy and procedure manual, I think it is a mistake. If someone is speaking for your organization to the entire industry, use caution. I also think there should be a policy for when you release product information or run ads on new product, something to the effect of not earlier than XX days before the product is set to be in our warehouse. Believe me, you won't miss a dollar of sales; all your key customers will get the private screening of your new program at the same time. They need to see it to make their purchasing decisions, so why also show your competitors that program so far in advance of shipping?

DRESS FOR SUCCESS?

**"What the hell is it with these $3,000 suits?
The man dresses better than Cuomo."**

Paul Castellano speaking about Gotti, *Gotti*

This topic is tricky given the trend towards casual dress, and certain industries, like tech and design, have become VERY casual.

They used to say look at how your boss dresses and use that as a guide for how you should dress. Not sure that is always solid advice as your boss might be a 22-year-old tech genius and you might be a 59-year-old finance executive. On the flip side, you are a 24-year-old junior associate and your boss is the 70-year-old CEO.

The need or right for individuality and self-expression is recognized and appreciated at most companies. The factors are probably the industry and your position. A neck tattoo does not work as well on a senior financial planner as it might for a self-employed industrial designer.

If you are not sure, think back to the smell test. You can always unleash your wild child self on the weekends.

Some of the classic bits of advice always work and still hold true.

Better to be overdressed than underdressed.

If you think you might be getting too trendy or pushing it, tone it down, as you probably are.

MEMO TO MANAGEMENT

Dress for success, not to infuriate.

WHAT IS YOUR HIT RATE?

"Even a broken clock is right twice a day."

Tony Soprano, *The Sopranos*

In many industries, they introduce hundreds of products a year; in some cases, thousands. At trade shows, buyers often walk into a booth, and the first words out of their mouths are "what's new?"

A CEO of a large company wanted to impress his customers with how many new products his company had developed for the trade show. He had buttons made up bearing the number 1800 and a statement to ask what it meant. He made everyone from his company wear the button. At the show, when prompted, the answer given was *this is how many new products we have at the show.* What the customers really wanted to know was *how many new products do you have that will make a difference in driving my sales and profits?* Most retailers will conclude that a minor adjustment to an existing item is not worth the effort for them to make a change to their current assortment, or the disruptions it would cause to their business. But hey, if not for insignificant product changes like that, the 1800 number would have been much lower. Customers are getting smarter about the actual cost of changing out one program for another and are demanding the change be valid and profitable.

When doing line extensions, be aware whether they are needed or just a churn that creates work instead of actual gain. If they are at a lower retail, meaning you need to sell more units, this approach needs to make sense. If they are at a lower margin than the item they are replacing, check the logic carefully. Ask yourself if any of your introductions are likely to move the needle in a meaningful way. Introducing one great item beats introducing 1800 meaningless ones.

MEMO TO MANAGEMENT

Create a product development hit rate report. Have it documented and updated quarterly, and let it run for a few years. If you can look back and see the results of products introduced for each of the last 5 or 10 years, what will they tell you? Make sure you include information that can be sorted in various ways to tell you different things—retails, product categories, materials, packaging, etc. This way you can determine if you have had more success at a certain price range, in a specific material, or with a particular product category. If there are any patterns to your successes or failures, you can focus on those to improve your future hit rates.

You should also indicate the marketing manager or department so each individual or department can have their own product development hit rate report. I can tell you when I instituted this in various places, the product development people hated it because there were now cold, hard numbers to evaluate. I was not doing it to throw anyone under the bus, but as a means of learning what we can do to improve our hit rate going forward by evaluating what worked and what did not work.

When I was a young marketing manager, each year I would learn something else about a particular product and kick myself for not knowing it earlier. I would say out loud that I should have thought of this last year. I mentioned this to a much older gentleman once who was working with us as a consultant, and he was what you would genuinely call an old codger from Maine. He never held back and was always on point.

He said, "That's why they didn't build a 1990 Cadillac in 1980."

WHEN YOUR HEAD SAYS ONE THING, AND YOUR HEART SAYS ANOTHER

"When did I ever refuse an accommodation?"

Don Corleone, *The Godfather*

When your customers put the squeeze on you, how you respond could determine if you make or miss your year, and if you keep or lose the customer. No pressure.

If the request stems from something you did wrong—you shipped late, the product had a defect, anything that was in your area of responsibility—the answer is an automatic yes.

But what if you did nothing wrong and the customer is just being unreasonable?

Maybe they have internal pressure. Maybe the buyer is trying to hit a number for his year-end bonus. Maybe they are just playing hard ball. But you did nothing wrong, and their request will wipe out a substantial portion of your profits and cause you great distress. What then? Best to talk this over with a few people in your organization. You want partners at this point. The salesperson will almost always recommend to do whatever the customer wants, so you need to have some other points of view to make an intelligent decision.

How important is the customer? Can you count on them for future years if you make their request happen? Can you count on that if you don't? Can you afford to do it, and what are the actual consequences to your company if you do it? What alternatives do you have?

These are the decisions that define a year and, sometimes, a career.

MEMO TO MANAGEMENT

There is only one Wal-Mart, one Costco, one Amazon. If the request is at all within the bounds of manageable, you need to make it work. But you don't always have to do it 100%. You can try to negotiate a way that satisfies the situation without taking on 100% of the burden. Maybe you time-phase it. Maybe you get something in return to counterbalance it. Maybe you offer 80% of their ask. Either way, it's better to take a hit and live to see another day.

IN HOUSE, OUT HOUSE

"I'm doing it myself, that's why it's so damn expensive."

Jimmy Hoffa, *Hoffa*

It makes sense to look at every department and do the math on keeping that department versus outsourcing that function.

Do the math not only on the cost, but on the time and the expertise, training, and quality of the work.

You should also look at the value of outsourcing certain parts of each function as well as the entire function.

This is how you should review the business as a whole. At home, you do the same thing. Is it worth my time and effort to cut my own lawn or is the cost to hire someone reasonable enough that I want that extra time to myself?

Outsourcing is available for basically every function of the business.

Within your own "to do" list, you need to determine how much to delegate to others and how much to do yourself. If you delegate, make sure you follow up and provide certain dates for check-in and update sessions so you don't have to worry if it is getting done. A good way to determine the quality of work your direct staff can handle is by giving some of them something you would normally do yourself. It gives you a good indication of who is potentially able to step up if you ever need to backfill your own position.

MEMO TO MANAGEMENT

Often the biggest disparity of the quality of work done in-house versus an outside agency is on the creative side. The designers, graphic artists, creative PR people, advertising executives, and packaging people often start their own firms, at least the really good ones. The beginners and career "middle of the roaders" tend to stay in a corporate environment rather than branching out on their own. Not always, but this is often the case.

Pending the level of quality you need in any of these creative areas, you may need to think of inside vs. outside for the job. It can be on a case by case basis with some inside and some outside or a shift to a total outsource model. If you offer outsource agencies the opportunity to bid on your total business, they should be able to get creative to make the arrangement work financially for both of you. Just one word of caution: there are turf issues, and if you leave the management of the outside agency totally to the head of your in-house department, make sure the in-house person is not more interested in sabotage than getting the best job done. Some people are more interested in undermining the outsource effort in what they determine as an act of survival. In these cases, make sure you are directly involved in all the update meetings and communication with the outsource agency.

CONFERENCE ROOM BULLY

**"The loudest one in the room
is the weakest one in the room."**

Frank Lucas, *The American Gangster*

Pick your spots and know when to speak.

Don't repeat what others have said just because you feel you need to say something.

If you have something constructive to say, go ahead. If not, keep quiet until you do. Don't try and dominate the conversation, and don't be afraid to ask others in the room questions. If you are not clear on the topic, the point or any detail, ask for clarification; chances are you are not the only person unclear on the issue.

When you have something to say that covers more than one point, mention that up front by saying: "I see three issues here, first is this, second is this, and third is that." It will let people know how many points there are and make it easy to follow your train of thought.

You will know the people who make valid points when you see other people taking notes of what is being said.

MEMO TO MANAGEMENT

> I have run meetings where certain people will speak and speak and speak. At some point, I actually interrupt and ask, "Can you tell me what point you are trying to make?" Funny, they usually tell me what their point was in around ten seconds, which makes you wonder why they were talking for ten minutes. Other times, they have gotten so twisted, they are not sure what their point is. If I don't get their point quickly and clearly, I stop them and point blank ask. Anyone who attends enough of my meetings quickly picks up on this, and the smart ones know to get to the point quickly. I know the rest of the attendees appreciate it when people follow this format. We have other things we can be doing.

PITCH TO BE RE-PITCHED

"One thing I learned from Pop was to try to think as people around you think, and on that basis, anything is possible."

Michael Corleone, *The Godfather*

You have your agenda, and that's fine. But the person on the other side of the table has their agenda, as well. Get to know their agenda, concerns, goals, issues, openings, as well as what their priorities are.

When Willie Sutton said he robbed banks because that was where the money was, similarly, selling should be as simple as presenting solutions that address the needs of your customer. Just make sure you know what those needs are.

MEMO TO MANAGEMENT

Smart sales associates know that when they make their presentation to a customer, sometimes their ultimate customer is not sitting in front of them at the meeting. The real customer might be the boss who is not in attendance. If you can gear your presentation so it has enough data and hits on enough of the customer's hot spots, your meeting attendee can turn around and use your presentation as their presentation to their boss. Your goal is to make that person look good to their boss. Their success and promotion, or earning their bonus, is your goal. If you hit on these, your product or service becomes more desirable.

SALES VS. PRODUCT

**"You can get further with a kind word and
 a gun than you can with just a kind word."**

Al Capone, *The Untouchables*

The salesperson thinks it was her relationship with the customer and how she handled the meeting that got the program placed.

The product development person thinks the product is great and any salesperson should have success as the product sells itself.

The salesperson returns from an unsuccessful meeting and tells her boss, "The product just isn't better than what is out there, and the customer has no interest."

The product development person reviews the unsuccessful meeting and is convinced the salesperson did not present the product correctly.

Does any of this sound familiar? All of it, I imagine.

You rarely win without both ends of the equation working.

I mentioned earlier the importance of sales preparation and advance planning, and I believe it should be a joint, collaborative effort. I have seen too many sales presentations done by the sales department in a vacuum. When the product development and marketing department see them, sometimes after the meeting, they rip them apart. Better to get that input up front so all sides agree that the best effort is being presented.

MEMO TO MANAGEMENT

Whenever there is an initial product launch of a significant new program to a major customer, have the development team go to the meeting and make the pitch. Don't leave that to the salesperson. The salesperson should guide the process so the right things are said and the wrong things are left unsaid—they know the customer. The development team knows the product, let each of them speak to what they know best.

OH, ENEMY, MY ENEMY

"Keep your friends close but your enemies closer"

Michael Corleone, *The Godfather*

If you don't know everything about your competitors, you are falling short.

It should go beyond their product, and with social media, you can do just that.

Gone are the days of limited information.

After you have done the SWOT analysis on your competitors, and after you have found the weakness in their strength, go further.

Do you have their full assortment on file? Do you line up your corresponding offering next to theirs to see where you fall short or where you beat them? Do you have action items planned to close each of these gaps? One company I knew kept a hall of shame of their own products they felt were inferior. It is good to do this direct comparison of your offering versus that of your top competitor.

Do you review LinkedIn or other sites to keep tabs on their employees in case you need to hire someone for a particular position?

Do you have photos of their in-store displays?

Have you performance-tested samples of their product versus your own?

Do you have a recap of online consumer reviews of their product so you know what consumers like most about your competitor's product as well as what they like least? This will help in your own development, in addition to selling against them.

MEMO TO MANAGEMENT

If you are in any type of "assortment" business, I suggest you find space for a "best-in-class" presentation somewhere in your building as a permanent set-up. It does not matter whether you are selling garden tools, cleaning products, kitchen tools, brochures, or building supplies. For each item in that assortment, there is a SKU from one supplier that is universally thought of as the best of the best. Pick each of these best-in-class SKUs and place them in your building. (Some may be your own items if you are lucky and good.) Next to that best-in-class item, place your own. Under both items, list the factors that separate the items. Be complete and include specs, performance analysis, durability testing, consumer reviews, aesthetics, ergonomics, pricing, warranty, packaging, etc. Be brutally honest. For each area in which you fall short, assign a person to correct it. List the action item and the due date for completion. One by one, your goal should be to be equal to or better than the best-in-class for each item in the assortment range.

SELLING VS. TALKING

"She questioned when she should have been silent, she probed when she should have ignored."

Don Clericuzio, *The Last Don*

Selling is a skill.

I believe in the step theory of selling.

The step theory of selling should be taught to anyone who marches into a customer's office and starts off by showing the product.

Follow these steps please:

1. Get their attention.
2. Get their interest.
3. Propose a solution.
4. Introduce the product.
5. Get their positive response.
6. Be quiet.

At each step, it is important to know when to talk, when to listen, and when to shut up. Most people show the product too soon.

And when you are talking, ask questions that get you somewhere other than a dead end. Certain questions will lead to a conversation and a back and forth that could actually lead to progress.

MEMO TO MANAGEMENT

Everyone who will someday deal with a customer should have some sales training. Often, the product development or marketing people who make presentations have no sales training or skills. Often, the people manning your booth at trade shows have no idea how to deal with customers. I have run role-playing exercises in-house with one person playing the role of a tough buyer and the other person trying to sell them our new product. I have done this in front of the entire department. It trains the non-selling staff on how to sell, and it helps sales anticipate questions and objections they are likely to encounter. Plus, it's fun and humorous, and everyone seems to enjoy it. If you can get everyone up to speed to be a salesperson, even if in a pinch-hitting role, the organization will benefit.

NO MEANS NO,
UNLESS YOU ARE SELLING

**"Never take no for an answer,
because if you will not take no for an answer,
eventually the answer comes back to yes."**

Bobby Ciaro, *Hoffa*

As I mentioned earlier, the goal is to avoid asking questions that get you a simple no, as it is harder to steer the conversation back to neutral or positive territory.

If you do get a no, you need to find out what is behind the no. Is it a no due to price, is it a no due to appearance or functionality? Perhaps it is duplicative of what you have already? What would need to change for the customer to have a different opinion?

If you get the response like, "I don't know, I just don't like it," you'll have to peel that onion back a few layers. You can peel until the customer gets aggravated, and then you need to back off.

People love to talk, and it's your job to get them talking. Once they do, it's your job to listen.

It drives staff crazy when sales return to the office with negative news and the salesperson can't tell the marketing and product development person the reason the buyer turned it down.

Sometimes you can simply ask, what would we have to do or change to gain your interest?

MEMO TO MANAGEMENT

Insist on written copies of meeting notes of every customer meeting. Have them distributed to everyone who has an interest. It gives the people who were not at the meeting a chance to participate in follow-up questions. Being in writing and widely distributed, it also avoids verbal miscommunication.

PART 2

NOW THAT YOU'RE IN CHARGE

CHAPTER 1

DEVELOP A PLAN THAT MAKES SENSE

There are four steps you should consider when starting a new position, or when it is time to hit the reset button in your current position.

STEP 1 – The Brand

STEP 2 – Initial Analysis/SWOT

STEP 3 – SKU Rationalization

STEP 4 – Strategic Planning

Since you have to start somewhere, start at the beginning. The beginning is the Brand.

STEP 1 – UNDERSTAND YOUR BRAND

Ask questions about your brand from both internal and external sources. What do your employees think? What does management think? Consumers? What about your wholesale customers? The board? Even amongst your own employees, different departments may have different opinions. The key emphasis at this point should be asking questions and listening. Follow up the answers you get with more questions; keep peeling the onion.

Brand Review
- Equity
- Awareness
- Positioning
- Channel Strategy
- Limitations
- Opportunities
- Tier Strategy – Price points and sub-brands

Equity

What value does your brand have? Be honest.

Inquire from multiple sources. Read consumer reviews and see what consumers who have actually purchased your product say about your brand and your products. Brands do not appeal to everyone; make sure you understand the segment of the market that your brand appeals to. Brand expansion almost always dilutes the brand. Consumers realize you don't need 28 types of mayonnaise. Brands become stronger with focus on what the brand stands for. Trying to chase every last dollar just dilutes the brand. In the long term, your brand will be stronger not trying to sell to every living person on the planet. It's hard to be everything to everybody.

Do you have brand equity?

- If your branded product is sitting on a shelf next to an identical, or apparently identical, alternative product, would the consumer pay any more for your branded product?
- If the two choices were priced the same, do you usually win?

Answer these two questions and then proceed from there.

KEY POINT

Stick to the core value of the brand and sell

Awareness

Do you think your brand has more awareness than it actually does? Is all awareness good? Everyone has heard of Cadillac, but try selling one to someone under 30. Be honest about your brand's awareness. Research can tell you what the brand's aided and unaided brand awareness is.

Where are you at in the competitive landscape? If you are the leader and want to crush upstarts, you can keep piling on the advertising. If you are new to the market, keep a narrow focus of attack, otherwise you are bound to lose.

Combine the results of brand equity and brand awareness and determine your next steps. Strong brand awareness and low equity are obviously not good. Strong equity and low awareness can be addressed via advertising. Like most things, it's not always black and white. How you assess and evaluate the relative strengths and weaknesses of equity and awareness will help shape your approach to brand building. Or dumping.

KEY POINT

> To become big; think small, act small, and attack small. Keep your focus narrow until you are no longer small.

Positioning

Be better, be first, be different.

While these three points have merits, the single most important thing any brand can be is the first-to-market. First-to-market opportunities are the jet fuel of growth. Being better or different by itself is no guarantee of success. Sometimes you really are first; other times your customers just think you are first. Both have the same effect. It can either be a monumental "first" or a slight improvement. Perhaps a point of differentiation can be packaged and presented as a "first." The size of the change is not as important as how that change is perceived. It can be simple and obvious.

Perhaps the response will be "Why didn't someone think of that before?" The best odds of brand success are when you position your brand as a first-to-market opportunity. The best way to be first is to create your own category, or subcategory, to be first in.

Let me repeat that.

KEY POINT

Your best odds of success are when you create your own category or subcategory.

Channel Strategy

Channel strategy is another way of saying don't try to be everything to everybody.

When you analyze your current sales, what do they tell you? Today, more and more, channel strategy is going straight to the consumer via the internet. Even if you do go straight to the consumer, what type of consumer are you likely to appeal to? Make sure you understand your targeted consumer, what they want and don't want. Do you need multiple brands for various channels of distribution? Are you going to get more bang for your buck staying focused on one specific customer base? Will you dilute the brand and your cash, time, and energy going in too many directions? Test your bandwidth for your limitations.

Do you have the knowledge and connections to sell outside of your comfort zone or are you setting yourself up for failure? Generally, the more focused you are, the better.

KEY POINT

> Do you alienate and ultimately erode your base by attempting to expand your appeal?

Limitations

Understand the limits of your brand.

Channel strategy MUST match the brand limits. Understanding the brand limits allows you to properly focus your resources on the areas that will have the highest chance of success.

KEY POINT

> Don't waste your time or energy on low probability areas.

Opportunities

Be clear where you are in the brand hierarchy and timeline. This will help determine the opportunities. Fading brand with an older and declining customer base? New "on trend" brand creating buzz and on a fast growth trajectory? Stale and barely holding on brand? New brand ready for launch?

What opportunities are not currently being addressed? Are they within the realistic scope of your brand?

If this leads you to uncover an opportunity that exists, but is not well suited for your brand, create a new brand.

KEY POINT

> If you determine an opportunity area for your brand, figure out how to package it as a "first" and capture the first-to-market share of market.

Tier strategy and sub-brands

Compare the price range of your brand or brands with your actual sales by price point. If your brand offers prices from $10 to $100 and 90% of your sales are within the $10 to $50 range, reevaluate your brand price strategy NOW. If the items at the unproductive price range are valid, figure out a new strategy. Whether that is to create a new brand, a new sub-brand, or re-package the message, doing something is needed.

When I was running the largest bakeware company in the United States, we had two quality levels of bakeware under the same brand. The higher end line had a sub-brand attached to it and did very little volume. The opening price point line basically did all the business. We put a different brand name on the higher priced line, and almost immediately it was placed with one of the largest retailers in the country.

Avoid too many sub-brands that don't offer significant meaning or differentiation. They don't bring anything to the table and weaken the brand in the long term.

KEY POINT

> Know the strength of your brand relative to sales productivity—understand both the sweet spot and limits.

STEP 2 – INITIAL ANALYSIS/SWOT

SWOT analysis: Strengths, Weaknesses, Opportunities, and Threats.

This one-page recap should lead to an action plan, not a piece of paper that gets read, filed and forgotten.

Focus your attention in the first 30 days on asking questions. Get opinions and do the brand analysis. THEN, do your SWOT.

Develop your SWOT and don't share it with anyone just yet.

After you complete the process outlined below, revisit you SWOT.

See how you feel about it after you have followed these steps: Have each department in the company create the following four SWOT recaps. Have them do it independently of one another.

1. For the entire company.
2. By brand, for each brand.
3. By product category, for each product category.

4. By channel of distribution, for each channel that is meaningful.

Each department in the company may have a different perception of the company.

Meet with each department after they have completed their initial attempt at the SWOT recaps. Make sure you have sufficient back and forth, asking questions to help analyze their initial thoughts and help develop their "final" versions.

It's always interesting to see how the sales department differs from marketing, and how customer service and production each have a unique point of view. Finance will predictably be numbers-driven. Once each department has a reasonable working document, have a meeting with all departments so each department can present their SWOT to the other departments. Then begin the process of compiling all these SWOT documents into one single document that represents the cumulative efforts of the company.

Allow enough time for these meetings—the discussions can get lively. The final document, with group participation and sign off, gives you a blueprint.

KEY POINT

> After the conclusion of SWOT analysis, you must develop an action plan and a timeline. It is also important to provide periodic group updates on progress at pre-determined, set intervals.

STEP 3 – SKU RATIONALIZATION

Unproductive SKUs (or services) will suck the life out of a company. Not to mention cash, time and energy.

Done correctly, SKU rationalization is a time-consuming and tedious process, but one that is totally necessary.

Information that needs to be included:

Sales dollars (for each of last three years)

Unit sales (for each of last three year)

Top three customers and sales (for each of last three years)

Current item inventory (both on hand and in process)

Product margins (for each of last three years)

MOQ by item (or minimum production run)

Any current in-stock related components or parts by item.

KEY POINT

> Sort the report three ways: in descending sales dollar order, in descending margin order, and by product category.

This triple sorting method shows the warts pretty quickly. Low margins can't hide. Slow sellers can't hide. Product duplication or overlapping SKUs also become obvious.

Make sure someone from each department attends these review meetings, preferably the department head. Sales, PD, Marketing, Operations, Customer Service, Production/Purchasing, and Finance all should have a voice and a chance to express their opinions.

Perhaps you are over-assorted in a given category. Pricing may not make sense. Possibly an item died and no one realized it. Check to see if only one customer buys an item and an effort should be made to switch them to another SKU. Is the sales department selling a low margin item when a similar, more profitable item can be substituted? Ask if customer service has received complaints on a certain item and no one acted on it. Perhaps production hates making a certain item for efficiency or quality reasons and it causes issues no one was aware of or corrected.

Conclude the meeting with action items and a timeline.

KEY POINT

This is a decision-making meeting. The meeting should be held annually if not twice a year.

STEP 4 – STRATEGIC PLANNING

Once you have completed the brand review, the SWOT analysis, and the SKU rationalization, it's time for some strategic planning. This does not need to be an overly long report, but it does need to lay out the road map for how you expect to grow the business. What direction do you want to take the company? What steps need to be taken to get there? As always, include an anticipated timeline.

Category Level

You'll need to make decisions at the category level whether or not to:

Stay

Exit

Expand/Contract/Change

And then you'll need to offer the rationale for each of those decisions.

Channel/Customer Review

What are the growth expectations if you stick to the current course?

Where do you see both category and customer growth going under your current direction?

Is it satisfactory? What needs to change to improve?

Trends/Issues/Opportunities

What impact will the current trends have on your business in the next few years?

Do not make the mistake of being overly optimistic.

Compare industry data to your product data to identify opportunity areas.

Identify where you underperform and overperform the industry.

Develop corrective action plans wherever you see an opportunity to increase performance.

KEY POINT

Try to see where the industry is going to be, not just where it currently is—what do the trend indicators tell you? Figure out where you need to be now AND going forward.

Review your sales by price point, material, brand, category and subcategory versus the industry. If you have multiple brands, does the hierarchy make sense?

Analyze your competitors' SWOT so you have a solid idea where to attack, and estimate the financial gain (and cost) to displace any of these competitors at a given retailer or market.

Document your penetration of each retailer's assortment—the percent of that assortment you own versus your competition.

Role play: How would you sell against yourself if you worked for the competition?

This will help you understand and identify your weak points. This role play exercise makes for an entertaining and informative workshop.

Rolling Three Year Product Plan

Develop a plan three years into the future. Realize year one is more solid than year two and much more solid than year three. Note that things will change. Adjustments will be made as you realize some plans will happen and some won't. New ideas or directions will emerge.

Break down each year's product plan into the three buckets listed below. It will help force you into recognizing what you are suggesting and the potential size of the return.

1. Line extensions
2. New category or subcategory
3. First-to-market opportunities

Try to keep this to a one-page recap for brevity and clarity. If your page is loaded with lots of line extensions and not much else, you have work to do.

Don't get hung up on whether the idea or item can actually be produced, or if you have all the details figured out just yet. It's fine to be a bit blue sky on this recap. These are ideas or goals, not concrete product plans. A good first step is to list what would be a great idea or item. Then worry about how to actually make it happen. At least you thought of something that could potentially be exciting. Don't be afraid to dream or think big. It's okay if you have to cross off ten ideas along the way to one big success. Sometimes a failed idea leads to another idea that will work.

KEY POINT

> First-to-market is the goal. Don't give up at the first setback. Figure out a way to adjust and keep it moving forward. However, if a project gets to the point where it's a time suck with little chance of success, move on and perhaps revisit it at a later date.

Annual Priorities

Priorities should be developed for the company as well as for individual departments.

Department priorities should be developed between the CEO and the department heads with a formal sign off from both.

The priorities should have both timelines and action items. Make the priorities as quantifiable as possible. Avoid generic, hard to measure statements. Make the priorities specific, concise, and strategic.

Review departmental priorities and status updates with all departments so the entire company is in the loop. Avoid having one department blaming the other for lack of progress. Priorities can be adjusted due to changing circumstances and needs.

KEY POINT

Don't overload any department with too many priorities. Stay focused and accomplish something.

AFTER THE FOUR POINT PLAN, IT'S TIME TO MANAGE

Daily or weekly – It can be impossible to manage all the data if you drown yourself in reports and paper. Figure out what key data points you need to know, and develop a one-page flash report. The flash report can be updated as needed. Take time to develop what works for you. This one pager can be your best friend.

Monthly – Develop a monthly management report and review it with all departments. Meet with key staff to review financials, inventory, sales, updates on annual priorities by department, and any current issues and opportunities.

Don't drown yourself in meetings or reports, but the above two reports should make life a bit easier.

CHAPTER 2

Sales Management

When it comes to the sales organization set up, I usually start by wanting to know two things:

1. My cost of sales by territory or account, and
2. Where the customers are located versus where the sales personnel responsible for these customers are located.

I can't imagine anything simpler from a sales management analysis, but this has been screwed up by more companies than I would have thought possible.

NOTE – The cost of sales chart assumes all sales are at the same gross margin dollars. If your sales margins vary by customer/territory, adjust the chart to allow for gross margin dollar variance.

COST OF SALES ANALYSIS

In-house Or Rep Group?	Rep Group/Sales Person	Annual $ Sales

Total Annual Cost to Company*	% Cost to Sales	Territory	Top Three Customers Volume/Location

*Total Cost to Company should include:
Salary/Commissions/Bonus/Benefits/T&E, etc.

SALES CUSTOMER VS. CUSTOMER LOCATION MAP/CHART

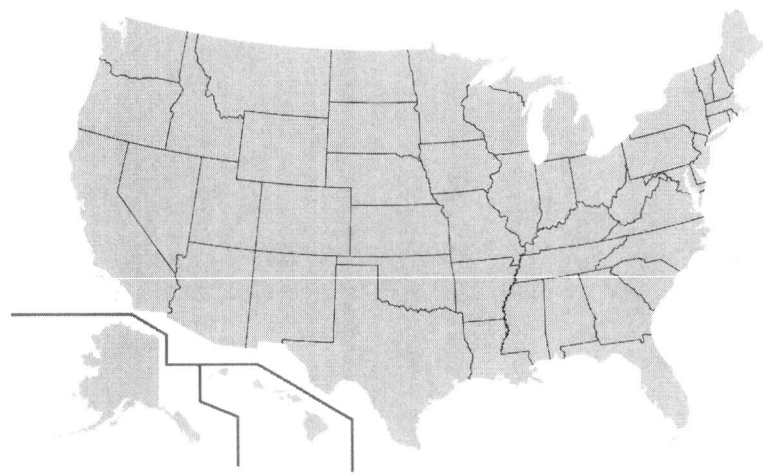

- Color Code each Rep Territory and Indicate Rep and $ Amount of Sales
- Pinpoint Location of each In-House Person and $ Amount of Sales
- Pinpoint Location of the "Top 20" Customers, $ Amount of Sales and Salesperson

The simplicity of having your salespeople located near the major customers to reduce travel cost and increase the frequency of customer contact is so basic, one would assume it's not necessary to mention it. One would assume wrongly in many cases.

Cost of sales by customer or territory should tell you if your sales cost and coverage is appropriately allocated. After analyzing the numbers, see if you need to make adjustments to your allocation of sales resources. Also, see if your salesperson who is producing adequate numbers for their territory is overly reliant on one or two customers, thereby producing good overall numbers but in actuality having several underdeveloped areas.

Dig Into The Sales Number

Sales staff will ALWAYS present their numbers in the best possible light.

The total sales number for a salesperson is important, but before you just accept that number, dig a bit deeper. If your company has six product categories, is the salesperson getting all their sales from only one or two of your six categories? If so, your product and marketing plans may suffer even though that salesperson is hitting their numbers.

SALES REP/SALESPERSON PERFORMANCE
BY PRODUCT CATEGORY REPORT

	SALESPERSON A		SALESPERSON B	
Category	$ Sales	% to Total	$ Sales	% to Total
Metal Gift				
Dinnerware				
Lighting				
Furniture				
Jewelry				
Kitchen				
Other				

Category	SALESPERSON C		SALESPERSON D	
	$ Sales	% to Total	$ Sales	% to Total
Metal Gift				
Dinnerware				
Lighting				
Furniture				
Jewelry				
Kitchen				
Other				

*The categories listed above are examples.
Please insert your own product categories.

MONTHLY REPORT

% to Total = the % to the total sales for that salesperson

If the report tells you some salespeople are killing it in a certain category, while other sales staff are having difficulty in that category, find out why. What is working for one person that is not working for the other? Even with salespeople producing great numbers, if they are not hitting on all product categories, they can probably do better. I have noticed in meetings when salespeople get a positive response, they stop selling. Sometimes they don't want to try to sell the buyer too much at one time. However, if they don't go back and represent the rest of the line at some point, it is possibly a lost opportunity.

I normally have a monthly key customer recap as part of the sales section of the monthly management meeting. I find having the numbers prepared the way I want to see them gives me a certain point of clarity before any sales "spin" is applied to the presentation.

MONTHLY KEY CUSTOMER RECAP

Retailer:

SALES

Current MO. Actual	Current MO. Budget	PY Month	YTD Sales

SALES

Budget YTD Sales	PYTD Sales	YTD +/- $/% to Budget

Also include in the report:
- Retailer sell-through and feedback
- Sales shipments and commentary

I want the basic numbers of monthly sales compared to budgeted monthly sales and prior year monthly sales. The same goes for YTD numbers. I also want to know two additional critical bits of information at the customer level:

1. Retail sell- through - Sales tells me what we shipped. I also want to know how the customer sold through during this time period. If their sell-through is off the charts, see if they need to adjust their forecast and whether we should adjust our production/purchase plan as well. If their sell-through is lagging, find out why and see if any downward adjustments need to be made to our plan. Keeping in mind a month is just a month, see if a trend develops. The commentary section should add clarity.

2. Sales shipments - What was our percent fill on their orders in this time period for that customer? If we show sales of $100, did we actually have orders for $125 that could have shipped? If so, I'd like to see why we left sales unshipped. Having both sales and operations in the monthly management meeting will give you both sides of the coin.

Sales By Channel Of Distribution

Make sure you document your sales by channel of distribution on a monthly basis and also YTD versus prior YTD. Significant increases/decreases by channel obviously need an explanation and possible adjustment to allocated resources.

Other Voices

Having a sales council can be helpful. Sometimes it can be beneficial to converse with a small group of key sales associates (whether internal or external sales personnel). This group can include personnel you don't normally have direct access to. Create a venue to free up additional voices and encourage input.

KEY POINT

> The biggest challenge is often finding people who will speak truth to power.

Inventory

Most of your cash is likely tied up in inventory.

Sometimes a report showing the inventory number does not get through to people. Perhaps they are just numbers on a page.

For a visual that tends to work, set up a warehouse walk through for your sales and marketing people, and have the warehouse manager conduct the walk through. Warehouse managers tend to be pretty direct individuals and are "tell it like it is" type people. Walking through a warehouse with the warehouse manager pointing out stacks of boxes that have not moved in a while is pretty impactful. The visual of boxes stacked up in row after row gets the message across better than any report could. The visual impact helps prevent the "out of sight, out of mind "thinking.

The single biggest surprise about inventory management is how many companies do not produce an aged inventory report. I find it unbelievable not to have this report.

KEY POINT

Dead wood in your inventory drains the cash you could be using to stock your best sellers.

Aged Inventory Report

Item	Description	Days in Stock since last Customer PO	Total Quantity in Stock

$ Value in Stock	Months of Supply on Hand	Any Open Supply Purchase Orders?

List in descending value of days in stock without PO

When you sort the aged inventory report in value of days in stock without a purchase order, it can get pretty scary. If that does not scare you enough, perhaps the months of supply on hand will do the trick.

Unless its wine you are stocking, the value of your inventory is not going up. There is no sense continuing to hold it. Reduce the price and move it out for whatever you can get. Your cash flow report will appreciate it.

KEY POINT

Inventory is cash.

CHAPTER 3

OPERATIONS

Customer deductions are a potential kill zone for your profits.

On a monthly basis I want a customer deductions report that tells me the following by customer:

1. Total deductions in dollars.
2. Dollar value of valid deductions.
3. Dollar value of unauthorized deductions.
4. Dollar value of valid deductions that were due to our own error.
5. What are we doing to correct the error that caused the deduction?
6. Follow up and status of getting the money back from the unauthorized deduction.

A common customer tactic is to keep asking for information to delay, delay, delay until you stop asking for the money back.

Make sure errors that caused a valid deduction are not self-inflicted and recurring. If they are, change procedures. If that does not work, change personnel.

KEY POINT

The longer you wait to follow up on unauthorized deductions, the harder it is to get your money back.

Customer Service

Treat customer service like your front line soldiers and make sure you know what they are hearing each day from sales and your customers.

Figure out how to get a reasonable recap from customer service that is organized into manageable buckets of information.

1. How many calls are they getting?
2. Note the topics and the percent breakdown.
3. If the issue is on our side, what corrective action was taken?
4. Did the appropriate follow up take place internally and externally?

KEY POINT

An occasional lunch with the customer service department is informational and appreciated by the customer service group as a perk and a chance to be heard.

Authority Levels And Approvals

Does every level in the organization know their authority level for each instance they will encounter in their role?

Properly setting this up avoids unnecessary work delays and uncertainty.

KEY POINT

Everyone should know their authority, and also who needs to sign off for the next level when the decision exceeds the authority level.

Budgeting Basics

Are you setting your top line forecasts by customer, channel and product category?

Are you comparing your actual line items to both budget and UPDATED forecast each month?

Is your timeline for budget development realistic? Who drives the process?

Are you updating your inventory accruals quarterly?

Are you updating your gross margin percent forecast by customer and channel quarterly?

If you are missing the top line numbers but expect to make it up later in the year, are you prone to running out of days in the year before your numbers catch up?

Are staff members submitting budgets with a higher percent increase in expenses than the company is projecting in top line growth?

Revenue Growth

Revenue growth opportunities should be viewed from two sides of the coin:

From the perspectives of both sales and product development.

Growth From The Sales Side Of The Coin

1. Growth opportunities with existing customers:

   - With your current customer via additional SKUs or better sell-through on existing items.
   - With your current customer/different department—any design changes, repacking, or additional use of items that broaden appeal to other departments.

- At your current customer, identify the weak sisters in their assortment and develop programs/cost to displace competitive items.

2. Growth opportunities with new customers in your existing channels:

- On an annual basis, create a "hit list" or "wish list" of customers you don't currently sell to and budget the estimated acquisition costs into your budget.
- Think long term. Adding key customers, even in existing channels, may take several years. Be consistent with your follow up; eventually a breakthrough will present itself.

3. Growth opportunities with customers in new channels of distributions:

- Is the channel identified and vetted?
- Do you have existing product suitable for this channel?
- Can your existing sales staff handle this channel?
- Do you have the sourcing or manufacturing bandwidth to handle the needed items?
- Do you have analysis on competitors you would need to displace?

4. Growth opportunities in export:

- Do you have the knowledge of local markets, competitors and any barrier to entry?

- Do you approach customers directly or indirectly through a local distributor?
- Are you attending exhibits in appropriate trade shows that give you access to the players in the desired export market?
- Can you ship your products directly from the source of manufacturing to the export market?

Growth From The Product Development Side Of The Coin

1. Base Level – Line extensions are the base level, and are the easy trap too many companies fall into. These are probably not driving any significant growth, and might cause operational issues from inventory and margin hits. This is slippery slope territory.

   - Challenge the line extension if you don't strongly feel it will produce incremental sales.
   - Challenge the team to drop existing SKUs for each line extension.
   - Make sure you subtract the loss of volume from existing SKUs in your forecast that might be negatively impacted by revenue from the added sales from the line extension.
   - If the line extension makes any existing items obsolete, make sure you calculate the cost of eliminating those items from inventory and customers shelves.

- Is the line extension at equal or greater margin than any SKU it might have a negative impact on?

KEY POINT

> With line extensions, are you adding sales or trading sales?

2. Mid-Level –
   - New product categories. This may require a new branding strategy. Beware of diluting you existing brand with too much expansion into adjacent categories.
   - Subcategories of existing product category. Check for any potential brand issue here as well.

KEY POINT

> The goal here is creating sales that are truly incremental

3. Top Shelf – First-to-Market Opportunities
   - First person at the party gets the largest slice of the pie, and generally keeps it. Even after copycats arrive.
   - First-to-market opportunities are margin enhancement vehicles.
   - If you are not really first, create the perception that you are first.

KEY POINT

> First-to-market opportunities are the holy grail of product development. The easiest to sell. Garner the largest market share. Represent truly incremental sales. Plus, you are free to price the product with sufficient margin.

Product Category Analysis

If you are in multiple product categories, consider grouping those categories into these buckets:

1. List the categories you consider CORE and go forward.
2. Which of these categories offer the most growth potential or most consistent revenue stream?
3. Are there potential exit categories?
4. Are there categories that are underperforming but have potential to improve? List the action items you need to take to make that happen.
5. Compare your sales by category to your inventory. Does the category produce 25% of your sales but is equal to 45% of your inventory dollars?
6. Compare your GM percent for each product category and the year over year trends on margin.
7. Develop a reasonable three-to five-year forecast by category and create priorities.

KEY POINT

The further in advance you can plan your exit strategy from any category, the more you can minimize the cost to exit with proactive steps to reduce inventory, transition customers, etc.

CHAPTER 4

Supplier Management

NOTE: Most of the comments in the supplier management section are geared toward an outsourcing model versus an in-house manufacturing model. However, some of the approaches can work for in-house manufacturing as well.

Create A Supplier Profile

In the initial potential supplier interview, you should create your supplier profile. A standard template can be created and used for each potential supplier. Some of the information that should be on the template includes:

- Management structure.
- Years in business.
- Volume.

- Geographic area of their sales—percent shipped to your market versus other countries.
- Top three customers and volume for each (if they will provide it, otherwise estimates).
- Core capabilities of their in-house manufacturing strengths.
- What part of the manufacturing process do they outsource?
- Lead time for initial orders.
- Lead time for reorders.
- Do they produce the molds/tools in-house?
- Their volume trend over the last five years.
- Number of production lines.
- Number of workers and number of shifts.
- Any seasonality to their production.
- Any particular strength of the supplier.
- Any particular weakness of the supplier.
- Analysis of their engineering and QC departments and processes.
- Review any key sub-factories they use for potential issues or backlogs.
- Have they passed retail audits from major retailers, or could they?
- What is the factory utilization rate? Minimum order quantities?

Factory Walk-Through

Check to see if what is on the supplier profile makes sense with what you see. Some other topics to take note of include:

- Number of production lines they have set up.
- How many of those production lines are currently in operation.
- Finished goods—what is staged for delivery?
- Master carton markings—check the name and addresses of who they are shipping to.
- Number of factory workers—does it seem to match the number on the profile?
- QC checkpoints—are they visible and in process? Have them explain it.
- Retail audits—have them show you the certificates.
- Raw materials and component parts—do they have sufficient supplies on hand, and what is the lead time for parts and materials?
- WIP (work in process)—what is currently being produced?

KEY POINT

Is there a production bottleneck that limits their output? If so, is there a workaround for that particular section? Perhaps stocking semi-finished goods in advance?

Explain Yourself

Make sure you explain who you are and what your company is about. Don't assume they know your mission. Sell the company to them. Explain the marketing angle of your product and business positioning.

Stress the financial stability and management/ownership structure of your organization. If English is not their first language, speak slowly and use a native speaking agent if needed. Leave time for questions and answers. Don't rush them. Stress your desire to build a long-term relationship. Make sure all your points are fully understood, and repeat if necessary.

Understand Their MOQs

Make sure you know all the component parts of their stated MOQs (Minimum Order Quantities). They might give you an MOQ of 3,000, but in actuality, there might be only one element of the BOM (Bill of Materials) that is driving that number. An example could be that the packaging has an MOQ of 3,000, but for the product they would accept an MOQ of 1,000. In that case, you can probably commit for the 3,000 units of packaging and get them to agree to ship 1,000 units of finished goods and hold the 2,000 balance of packaging units.

KEY POINT

> Find out if there is a single part of the BOM that is increasing the MOQ and perhaps there is a work around to lower the MOQ.

Price Negotiations

Multiple Bids

The goal should be at least three bids on each project. Make sure the quotes are in writing with all details clearly spelled out regarding BOMs and product specs. Don't be fooled by a lowball quote that might not have the same quality level as the other quotes. Make sure all quotes are valid. It's also a good idea to ask the supplier if they have any ideas to reduce costs. Perhaps you can live with their suggestions.

KEY POINT

> Take note of currency exchange rates and raw material costs at the time of the quotes, and add this to your copy of the quote for YOUR OWN reference. You can refer back to this if exchange rates or raw material costs change significantly at a later date in your favor. But beware, this can swing both ways.

Understand The Bill Of Materials

Preferably, you have multiple quotes, all are broken out into the various BOM that make up each part of the product, and you have a separate cost for each element of the BOM.

Compare the detailed BOM from each supplier to look for any outliers. If one supplier is considerably lower on a certain element of the BOM, find out why. Perhaps they are more efficient in that part of the manufacturing process. Or perhaps the other supplier is simply charging too much.

KEY POINT

One tactic is to take the lowest cost from each supplier for each part of the BOM and see if that becomes a realistic target cost for the finished goods cost.

Changes To Specs Or BOM

- Learn the increase or decrease to a product cost when altering the specs.
- Don't change specs before understanding the cost impact.
- Understand the cost ramifications on any changes to the BOM.
- Compare cost changes from factory to factory for similar changes to specs or BOM.

Menu Pricing

It can be helpful to create a menu of pricing options on a chart so if you change the material gauge by a certain amount, you know what the cost impact will be. Sometime even a simple item can have many variations in specs and materials—it's best to know the impact of each material option, each gauge, each packaging type, etc. It makes you more knowledgeable on your pricing options. The cost impact can be stated in currency or a percent change.

Targeting Cost Reductions

Avoid offering the first volley on a target cost; you might aim high.

The BOM should be helpful. Use it for analysis on pricing requests rather than simply asking for a lower price. Offer an analysis on why you feel the price is too high. Make sure you get a satisfactory explanation for their pricing structure. Again, the lowest common denominator among supplier costs by BOM parts should be used to your advantage.

KEY POINT

Who is asking for the quote and who is providing it? Titles help; the higher ranking person can generally secure a better price than a lower level staff member. Also, if the sales manager is providing the quote instead of the factory owner, there is probably additional room in the price.

In-person negotiations tend to be more productive than long distance requests. When it's time to get serious, it's best to be there.

It is much easier to negotiate the best price when you are ready to make a volume commitment. A firm purchase order in hand usually gets everyone's attention and cooperation.

If, in fact, you have negotiated the price for standard volume levels or MOQs, and you are fortunate to land a big account that has placed a large volume order with your company, do not simply place the purchase order with the supplier.

KEY POINT

If you have a large volume order or commitment in hand from a major customer, don't place the purchase order just yet. Advise the supplier that you have an excellent CHANCE of securing a large volume order of XX pieces, but the customer requires a better price, and if you can provide a cost reduction of XX%, you can guarantee the supplier the order. You have nothing to lose by asking.

Tooling Costs

If you are creating an item from scratch that requires a tooling investment, there are options for handling the tooling cost.

If you have a relationship and a history with the supplier, they should be open to paying for all or a portion of the costs. It helps to get the supplier excited about the volume potential; if they see the potential, they are more likely to invest.

if you must pay tooling, minimize the initial cash outlay. Factories are open to a downpayment and payment per piece, amortizing the cost of tooling per piece ordered over a period of time.

KEY POINT

> If you are forced to pay the tooling, try and negotiate a pay-back of all or part of your tooling expense after you reach a certain level of unit volume ordered and shipped. Negotiate this upfront.

If the supplier pays for the tooling, they are likely adding in a per piece amortization rate to the product cost. Find out at what volume level you can get a cost reduction after the item is fully amortized.

Models And Prototypes

If you must pay for models or prototypes, it is possible that you can negotiate a payback of this cost. You can usually do this upfront with a written agreement before any purchase orders are placed.

KEY POINT

Memo to supplier: We will be paying for the model of this item; however, if we should select your factory for this business and we place a purchase order with you within 12 months of the model date, we will deduct the cost of the model from the value of the first purchase order. Please confirm acceptance of these terms.

Things Not To Say Or Put In Writing

- We have decided to add a laser etching to the product and would like you to advise us of the additional cost.
- Your quote was for an MOQ of 5,000. Please advise us of the cost for a 1,000 MOQ.
- I am sending you a sample from competitor X, and I'd like you to make our handle the same as theirs.
- We are concerned that our design is too close to the competitor's existing item, which is covered by a patent, so we may change it slightly.

KEY POINT

> Don't mention any specific competitor or acknowledge you
> might be infringing on someone's patent—it will be used
> against you in discovery.

If you are actually sending a supplier a competitor's sample, it's safer to simply advise, "I'm sending you a sample for
you to review. When you receive this sample, please call me to
discuss."

KEY POINT

> Don't lead with your chin. Don't open the door to make it
> easy for the supplier to quote you a higher price, don't in-
> vite the price increase.

Supplier Agreement

Take careful consideration in developing a supplier agreement before purchase orders and actual business commence.
Consider all the various pitfalls, and detail who is responsible
and how each issue will be handled. It's okay to have an initial
approach where you are asking for certain elements that the
supplier may object to. It's a starting point, and you can expect
some negotiation—assuming they read it.

After you have an agreement, both sides should sign and date the agreement. Please be fully aware that a signed document with a supplier is not ironclad and will most likely never lead to legal action. In reality, it's a written guideline addressing how you expect each side to behave. Compliance is not guaranteed, and it's usually impossible to force one side to abide by the agreement if they have a change of heart. It is, however, something you can point to, and it's better than nothing.

Of course, legal action and recourse also depend on if you want to maintain an ongoing relationship with the supplier. If both sides feel they need each other, it helps to resolve conflict. Otherwise, it becomes disaster city if neither party has intentions to continue the relationship.

Some of the items to cover in a supplier agreement include:

- Payment terms.
- Anticipated lead time for first order and reorders.
- How to handle projections.
- Whether they will stock parts and raw material or inventory for your anticipated shipments.
- Plan to handle defective claims.
- Any free goods for sales samples.
- Who is responsible for expedited shipping costs if the supplier is late by more than an acceptable delay.

- Define each party's responsibility to cover the cost of molds and tooling. If you must pay for the tooling yourself, attempt to amortize as much of the cost as possible over a period of time with each piece ordered.

CHAPTER 5

Product Development

You decide to enter a certain product category or expand your existing offering in a particular category. You do your market research, taking note of what already exists and what you will be competing against.

Take note of what you see. More importantly, take note of what you don't see. You need to see in your mind's eye what your eyes do not see. Some people can do it, most can't.

It's the same with data. Consumer reviews, surveys, and other input will tell you certain useful data points. But consider that most likely EVERYONE has access to the same data. If you can't read between the lines or connect the dots, you won't get any more out of this data than anyone else does. The person who connects the dots creates the most unique product—same data, different results from different people.

It's like that scene from the movie *City Slickers*. Billy Crystal is trying to teach Daniel Stern how to work a VCR, but Daniel just does not get it. Finally, Bruno Kirby gets so annoyed, he yells, "He doesn't get it, he'll never get it, by now the cows could do it." It's the same with some marketing managers. You can shove the data down their throats, and some people will never connect the dots. They just take the data at face value. Trying to teach people to do this is very difficult, if not impossible. You either have a talent for product development or you don't. Having the wrong people in this position is the kiss of death.

Sometimes there is no data. No surveys. You can still look for an untapped opportunity. Or perhaps you see what no one else sees, additional potential for an existing item that can be realized with some modifications. Remember the three-year product plan and the buckets for grouping your development. They will remind you to steer towards first-to-market opportunities.

Embrace Problems

It's a cliché, but the "find a problem and solve it "approach can happen. Problems can be your best friend if you work in product development. It does not have to be the cure for cancer. Any small problem can present an opportunity.

Years ago, I was looking for a bottle opener. I had a large gadget drawer in my kitchen, and it took forever to find the bottle opener, which I found annoying. The tool jug on the counter was basically the same as every other tool jug on the market, a round ceramic cylinder with tall tools in the center. I took a Quaker Oats container, cut it up, and added fins and smaller outer pockets for small gadgets with the tall tools in the center section. I added hooks between the smaller outer pockets, which is where that bottle opener was soon to be hanging, along with other gadgets. This item became a revolving tool and gadget organizer that was sold filled with the tools and gadgets. We sold over $7 million within the first 12 months on the market—basically because I was annoyed at how long it took to find a bottle opener. That was the extent of the data or study involved. My rough model and horrible drawing took an hour, then an outside designer made it look proper, and we were off and running.

Don't Fear Failure

Fail up. Failure can lead to your biggest success. When you fail, it means you're trying. You need to deal with the failure and see where it takes you. Don't assume it's a dead end. Keep going, but try a different route.

Years ago, we were in the enamel on steel tea kettle business. We were not the market leader; we were number two behind a company called Copco. Copco had fantastic distribution and basically owned the department store business—the bulk of the business at that time—solid color whistling tea kettles that retailed for $19.99. So, of course, we tried to get that business. We developed designs that we thought were just as nice, added a feature or two, and tried to undercut the pricing. It was like banging our heads against the wall. We got nowhere. So eventually, I looked at patterned kettles, thinking that would be easier, since I was a colossal failure at the solid color business. I was staring at kettles with pictures of cows and chickens decaled onto the body, and I thought what if, instead of just putting a picture of the animal onto the kettle, I tried to make the kettle shaped like the animal? This had been done for many years with tea pots, which were ceramic, and ceramic material could be made into any shape. Kettles, however, were formed metal and could only be in simple shapes. So we made an animal's head out of heat resistant plastic, put it over the spout of the kettle, and painted the animal's body onto the body of the kettle. We added a tail on the back of the kettle body for good measure.

Thus, the first novelty tea kettles were born, and we named the collection NovelTeas.

The cow was called Tea Cattle, the Rooster Tea Bird, and the Pig Pork Tea Pig. This silly story has a moral. We did $10 million in sales in this category at MUCH higher margins than we would have made in solid color tea kettles had our failed attempt to secure that business been successful. Instead of trying to sell a group of kettles at $19.99 retail with low margin, we found success selling a group at $29.99 retail with high margins.

KEY POINT

> There is power in creating a category that is first-to-market. If we had not failed in trying to place solid color kettles, I don't know if we would have created NovelTeas.

The Power of "What If?" And "Why?"

Think like a four-year-old. If you are constantly asking why was it done that way, or what if we tried it this way, it could eventually lead you down a road to a new development. Don't be afraid to ask questions. Sometimes there is no good reason why things are done a certain way, and the situation is ripe for a change.

What if we made it larger?

What if we made it smaller?

Easier to clean?

Easier to assemble?

Increased power?

Multi-functional?

Safer?

Easier to use?

Added improved storage and organization?

Better looking? Better performing?

More comfortable?

What are consumers saying they dislike about existing products? Use those comments to explore new possibilities.

Sometimes It's Right In Front Of You

I joined a high-end designer metal gift company as CEO. The company was in the metal giftware and serveware business. In reviewing the top 20 items, I noticed there were two items that showed up in the top 10 year after year. These two items had a small part made from wood, with the rest of the item made of the company's signature metal. When I asked about it, no one thought it had any particular significance. These same two items had remained unchanged for years; they just kept chugging along. These were the only two items in the company that had wood combined with the metal. There was a wood tray with small metal condiment bowls, and a wood chip bowl with a metal dip cup. I made these observations:

- The addition of wood to the metal added a "warmth" to the hard metal.
- Visually, the combination was appealing.
- In analyzing the bill of material, wood cost less than metal, so you could create the impression of added perceived value, especially if you used more wood than metal in the item.
- A bridal gift survey I read suggested that a top item requested by brides was an oversized wood salad bowl.

Shortly after a brief study period, I added an entire category of around 20 items that combined wood and metal. This very quickly became our largest selling category and raised sales and profits for the company in a dramatic fashion.

Side note: my own staff strenuously objected to the wood salad bowl (with metal servers) as they felt we were a metal company and this item, according to their logic, was mainly a wood item with metal accent. They felt I violated the core mission of the company. How did it work out? The top two selling items in the company for each of the next five years were wood salad bowls. Turns out people viewed us as a giftware design company, not just a metal company.

KEY POINT

> We presented this as a category of its own, creating a first-to-market opportunity. Plus, it increased our "footprint" at retail as this was seen as its own category.

On another occasion, I was managing the largest cutlery supplier in the United States. In reviewing sales shortly after I joined, the marketing manager walked me through our part of a major retailer's assortment. She pointed out their best-selling knife block set from us. This particular set, instead of including a sharpening steel, had a built-in manual sharpening slot. The slot was built into the block so the consumer simply inserted the knife into this slot to sharpen the blade. I asked how this set did at other retailers. She replied it was the only block of this type the company offered, and we had not placed it with any other retailer. I asked why we didn't expand it to all retailers. She felt perhaps it wasn't the sharpening slot that was driving sales, but the color of the handle. I dismissed that logic and expanded this type set to all retailers and it became a best seller. I knew a fraction about cutlery compared with what the marketing manager knew, but I knew enough not to argue with success.

KEY POINT

> We developed a separate branding strategy for the expansion. It became a best-selling line. More on cutlery later.

Early in my career, I was president of a housewares company that had a cleaning products division that did around $40 million in sales. This division had a full assortment of cleaning products for home and also for the professional. One of the better selling SKUs was a wood brush used for coating in commercial applications. There was absolutely nothing remarkable about this item. A large brush with wood handle, the end of the wood handle was painted red. It was the only item in the entire division that had red on the handle. When I asked why it sold well, the reply was a guess, but perhaps the brush was easy to locate on the job due to the red marking. I suggested making a full line of cleaning products with red accents and creating a brand name to reinforce the red aspect. I was given such a lukewarm reaction from the established people at this division, I let it slide and never developed it. I should have insisted we follow up on my thought. I was not comfortable enough in my new position to insist, but I should have. Live and learn.

KEY POINT

> Don't ignore your ideas, act on them to see where they take you.

Manage Via A KES

Once you have done research to actually develop an item, make sure you create a template that acts as your Key Event Schedule (KES). This KES needs to document each step you need to complete in the development process. If it needs to be done, it needs to be on your KES. Add dates and who is responsible.

CHAPTER 6

EVERYDAY SOLUTIONS

I was in the early stages of planning my retirement when a former business associate approached me about joining a startup that he was planning to launch. There was no acceptable name for the company; therefore, no logo. There was no product line planned. No designs. No plan to enter any particular product category. The assumption was that it would be in categories we had prior experience with. This was during the onset of COVID-19, so there was no travel. Since we had no staff, I would be working alone from the home office. Naturally, I accepted.

Sounded easy enough.

My task was to figure out what the company would make. What product categories? What products? What would we call the company, and how would we position it?

The name and logo we settled on is:

EVERYDAY **SOLUTIONS**

I had several ideas for paper towel holders, and I'll explain two of them.

Please note: I am not using any of these items as an example of anything spectacular, even though I like the items quite a bit. I am simply using them as examples of how you can differentiate a product in the concept and development phase to do something that has not been done before. FIRST-TO-MARKET.

Paper towel holders are a low-tech kitchen staple. Practically every house in America has at least one. They have been around forever.

At its basic form, they have a center pole and a base. Some have added features. Some might have a ratchet mechanism to keep the paper towels from unraveling too freely. Others have a tension arm that works on a spring and maintains contact with the paper towels as the roll decreases in size.

I noticed that the models with the spring-loaded tension arm made the tension arm in a very mechanical design. I thought we could have some fun with that function. I added a stainless steel dog on the base (and also a cat) and made the tension arm into the dog's tail. It functions the same as other units with a tension arm, but adds a decorative element. It helps that there are MILLIONS of dog and cat owners who buy lots of dog-and cat-themed items. We named these the Woof and Meow paper towel holders.

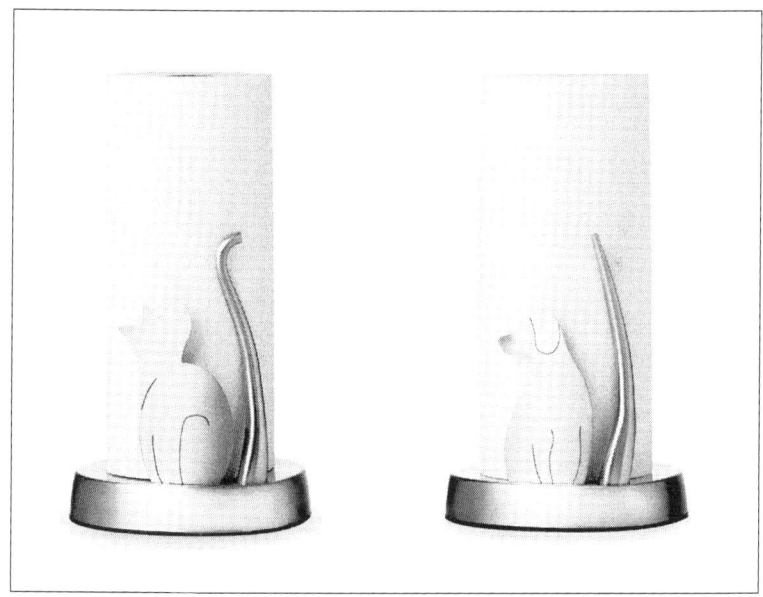

Another opportunity I wanted to explore was incorporating a spray bottle into the pole of the paper towel holder. Why? Because when I used the paper towels, I also grabbed the Windex or sanitizing spray at the same time, and I was always reaching for the spray bottle. I realized the center pole only needed to be a few inches tall off the base to hold the roll of paper towels. So we created the SPRAY paper towel holder. It's super convenient as the cleaner is always where you need it, and it's good for the environment as you can reduce the number of spray bottles you purchase and buy the larger refill bottles.

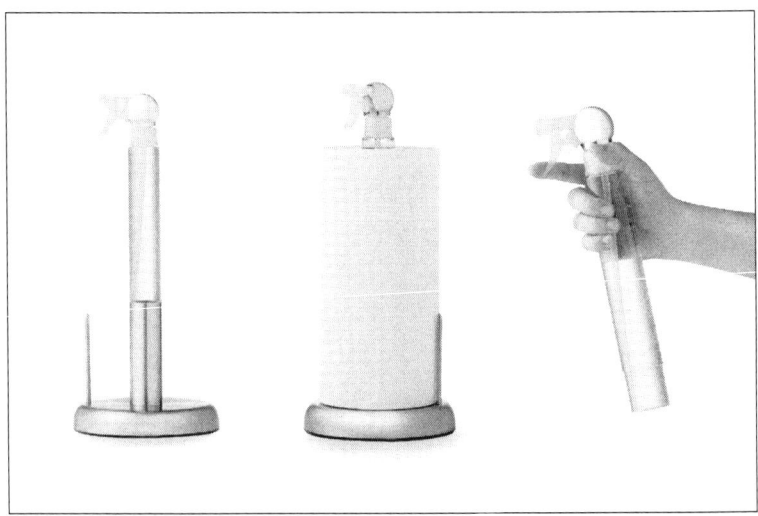

I was taking a bowl of soup out of the microwave and cursing at how hot the bowl was and how difficult it was to carry. This made me realize it was crazy that this was not addressed. I have seen bowls on the market with little helper handles, so I started with that thought. I then realized that silicone is heat resistant and would not get hot in the microwave. We designed these helper handles on both sides of the bowls and made a silicone sleeve to go over it. The silicone is designed for a snug fit and is attached with a glue that will hold up in the dishwasher. After I received my first samples, I used them all the time and loved them. Since I used them regularly, we called them Everyday

Bowls. They are sized for individual servings and work well for soup, stew, pasta, Chinese food, you name it. I joked around with the saying, "In a microwave, the bowls get hot, the handles do not." We wound up putting that on the box. I kept thinking this must have been done before, but as hard as I tried to find this idea on the market, I could not locate it. The saying, "Why didn't someone think of this before?" could apply here.

6" Bowl   8" Bowl

I am positive that pretty much no one thinks about a spoon rest, ever. Except one day, I did. Many people have a spoon rest on their counter. When you need it, it's right there. Have a dirty spoon to put down? That little sucker comes in handy. But for some reason, people are less likely to keep a trivet on their counter. I thought it would be neat to combine these two functions into one item. Thus the spoon rest/trivet. It gives you added function without any major fuss. Not much downside there. Again, first-to-market. Also, it is dishwasher safe, made of stainless steel so it won't break, and has nonslip grips on top and bottom. Simple and effective.

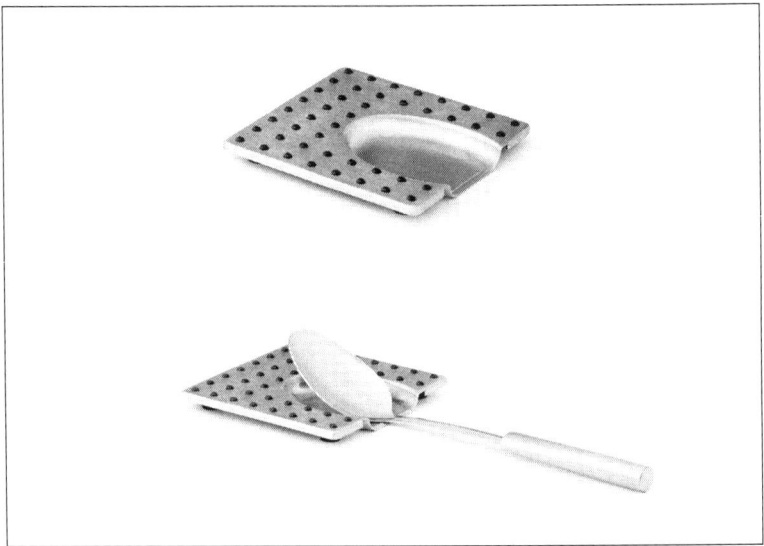

A peppermill is another item that is in practically every home. There used to be a significant difference in the quality of one mill to the other as the metal gears came in different quality levels. That has faded into oblivion as most mills now have switched to durable ceramic gears, and the playing field for quality has evened out. So other than shape, how to differentiate? It has always bugged me when it was time to refill the peppermill. It's a pain to take that small screw off the top, and you curse when you drop it and have to bend over to find it on the floor. On top of that, the inside of the mill is designed for the peppercorns to have to enter the mill single file. So an easy to fill pepper-mill made sense to me. We developed the EZ-PUSH-TO-FILL PEPPERMILL, the fastest and easiest peppermill refill system. I realize this is not Nobel peace prize level stuff, but hey, if it makes life easier, why not?

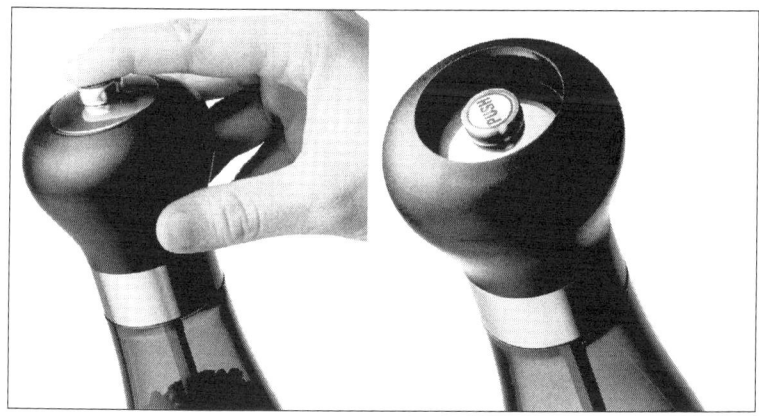

Push to open

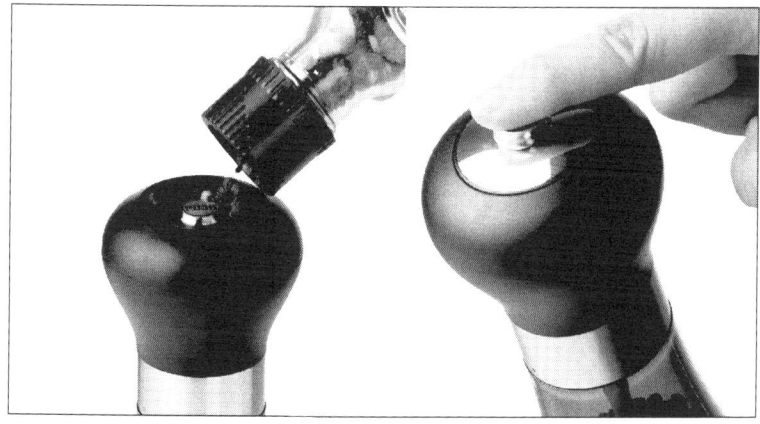

Fill and close

I previously mentioned a plastic gadget and tool organizer that was on the market decades ago and sold quite well. I decided it was time for a new generation. Instead of a plastic body, this is made from stoneware. The tools are stainless steel. It revolves and holds a 14-piece set. I expect it to also do well. Storage and organization are always in style.

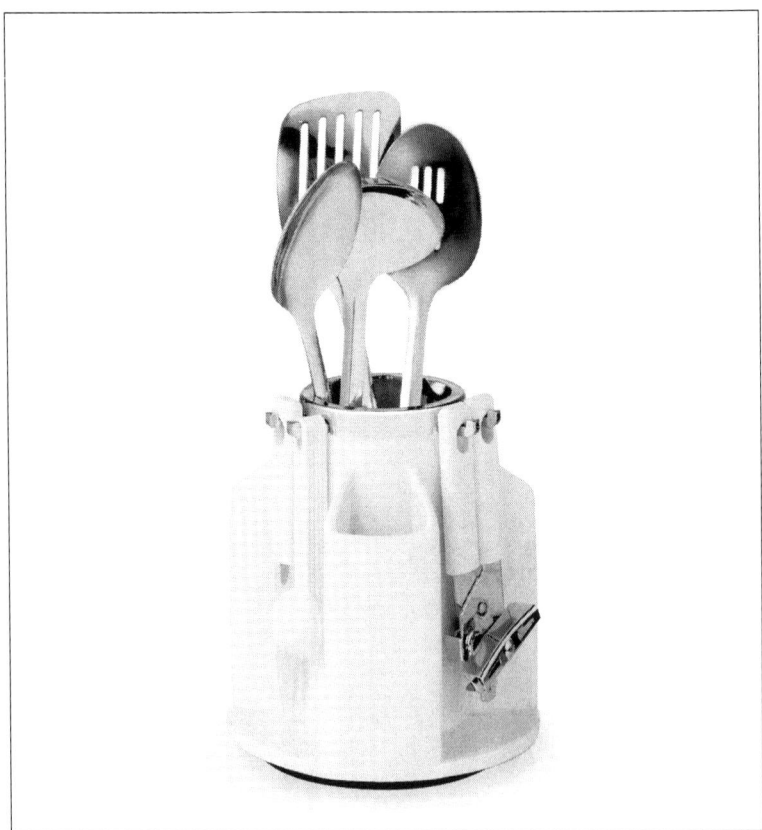

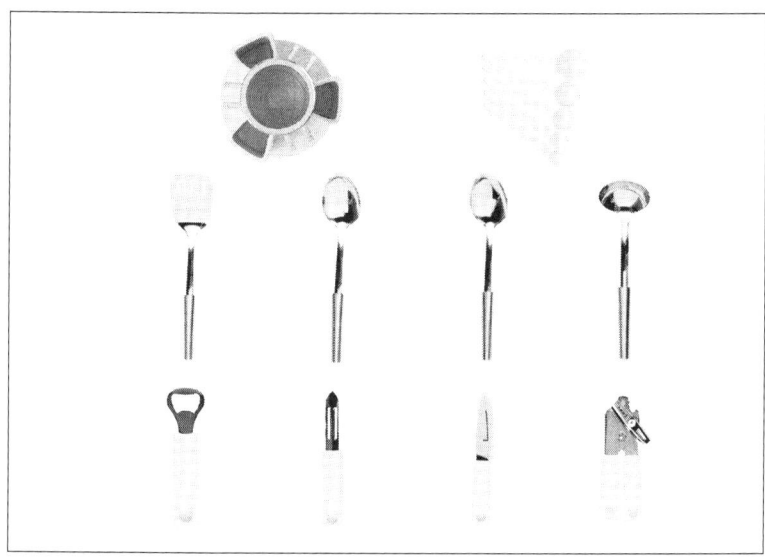

More On Cutlery

Years ago, there was a published report in an industry trade paper about the number one complaint consumers had with their knives. Their main beef, it turns out, was that their knives did not stay sharp. Yet—and this is the amazing part of the same survey—most people, it turns out, did not even bother to attempt to sharpen their knives. So their inaction helped cause and reinforce their number one complaint. Logical? Of course not, but it is fantastic information and was publicly available as it was printed in a trade paper.

Kitchen knives have been sold in wood blocks for around 50 years or so, and for almost all that time, the "at home" options to sharpen those knives were to use a sharpening steel, a sharpening stone, a manual knife sharpener or to drag out an electric sharpener. A few years ago, knife blocks, which sometimes had a single built-in ceramic knife sharpener, were altered to put that ceramic "V" shape manual sharpener into multiple slots instead of just one slot. These were now promoted as "self-sharpening knives," the theory being that every time you removed or replaced the knife, it would go through the manual "V" shaped ceramic sharpener and would sharpen itself. Sounds good in theory. However, it did have some drawbacks.

You do not effectively sharpen the knife with one pass through a manual sharpener. Most instructions for manual sharpeners recommend to pass the knife through the sharpener four to six times.

It is not necessary to sharpen your knife each time you use it, and each time you sharpen the knife, it takes off some metal.

What about the metal shavings? In these self-sharpening blocks, where the metal shavings go is a mystery.

Instructions for knife sharpeners say to wash and dry your knife after each time you sharpen the blade to remove loose metal shavings. So each time you take the knife out of a "self-sharpener" block, technically you should wash and dry the knife EVEN THOUGH you washed and dried it before you put it in the block. Is this a time saver? Hardly. Plus, do most people remember to wash and dry the knife EVERY TIME they remove it from the block? Consumers probably wind up using a knife on their food that contains loose metal shavings. Fantastic.

On top of that, the knife does not get very sharp with these types of systems; they just keep from getting dull.

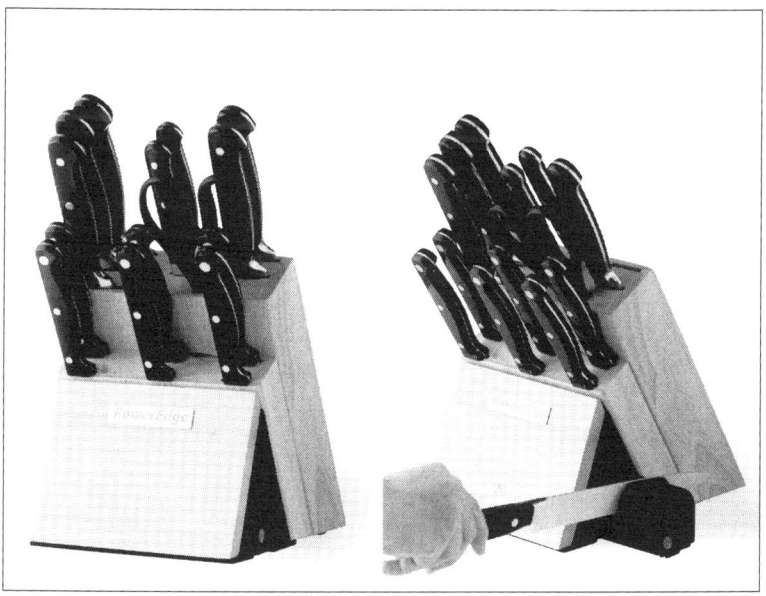

What To Do?

You can buy a separate electric knife sharpener and take it out whenever you need to sharpen your knives. These sharpeners do a splendid job. Storing this item and taking it out to use is not the most convenient option.

So we decided to create the world's first wood knife block with built-in electric knife sharpener. The design was created so you would not even know the electric sharpener was in the wood block. It is hidden and pops out with the touch of a finger, and it closes the same way. The electric cord on the back of the block (most blocks sit on the counter in front of an outlet) is also removable if you prefer to store the cord in a drawer. The unit is UL and CUL approved. Also, there is a magnet inside the sharpener which catches any metal shavings, and you can just clean the magnet periodically. The electric sharpener holds the blade at the correct angle and a few passes sharpens the blade correctly and properly. YOU decide when to sharpen your knives, the knives don't have loose metal shavings with each use, and you don't have to wash them before each use.

CHAPTER 7

DEVELOP YOUR MANAGEMENT APPROACH

Over time, managers develop their management style. Hopefully, you become a leader and a mentor, and not just someone with the big title. These are the traits and qualities that separate you from being just a suit and make you an inspirational figure in your organization.

For what it's worth, here are some of the guidelines that I have set for myself; evaluate my approach and develop your own set of rules as it's hard to be someone you are not. People see through insincerity and phoniness pretty quickly.

Four Guiding Principles:

1. Gather Intelligence
2. Become a Disciple of the Cs

3. Lead and Mentor

4. Follow the Money

Gather Intelligence

- Gather opinions PLUS data
- Compile market trends
- Read consumer reviews
- Study industry surveys
- Request wholesale buyers' input
- Maintain customer service logs
- Value your own employees who speak truth to power

KEY POINT

When you have enough input from various sources, see if there is a theme or trend. It might be between the lines or just beneath the surface.

Become A Disciple Of The Cs

I can describe your job in six words that begin with the letter C:

- Conductor
- Communicator
- Collaborator
- Coordinator
- Connecter
- Consequences

KEY POINT

> If you are not any good at communicating, connecting, coordinating, collaborating, conducting, or dealing with consequences, you are likely going to STINK at your job.

Lead And Mentor

The business is not necessarily a democracy. Often, one person needs to make the tough decision. However, it does take a team to succeed.

It helps to:

- Build consensus on priorities, timelines, and action items.
- Solicit feedback.
- Believe in and support training.

KEY POINT

> Having the boss's title does not automatically make you the leader or a mentor. One needs to be earned, and the other requires effort and interest on your part.

Follow The Money

Some money is out in the open waving a flag, and some is a bit harder to find.

OUT IN THE OPEN
- Selling prices
- Purchase prices
- Expenses

Selling prices – Salespeople HATE raising prices on their customers. Sometimes it has to be done, just don't lose the business. The challenge is not damaging your business when discussing a price increase, but sometimes you have no choice. Make sure the product can withstand any adjustment to the retail price point. It helps if your position is strong and your product unique. If you can be replaced at the drop of a hat, it gets tricky.

Purchase price – Often, the single most important factor in your profitability is what you pay your suppliers. Negotiate upfront like crazy. You have little to no control over most factors in the cost chain—freight rates, duties, etc. You do have some degree of say in what you pay for the product, or the first cost of the goods.

Expenses – Funny how in times of catastrophe you can manage your budget on a reduced level of funding. Why not try doing that to a degree in better times as well? You find out quickly what you can live without.

MONEY IN THE SHADOWS
- Supplier terms
- Customer terms
- Minimum Order Quantities (MOQ)
- Deductions and claims

Supplier terms – How many days your suppliers give you to pay has a direct connection to cash flow. Some people try to go from net 30 to net 60 or net 90. But if you strike out going to the next level, don't accept it. Go back with a mid-level option of net 45 or 75 and get a bit of a cash flow break.

Other less obvious supplier terms can help as well; can you negotiate a few free sales samples? Can you negotiate free freight on sales samples? Can you negotiate the cost of testing off tool samples? Have the supplier pay for the molds or tooling? A series of small concessions can add up across a larger number of items over a period of time.

Customer terms – Customers want to pay as slowly as possible, and whatever terms you give a customer for payment, it's pretty much a given that they will generally pay around 15 days later than their stated terms.

MOQ's – Consider the supplier who gives you a minimum order quantity of 2,000 pieces. Consider if all your suppliers have an

MOQ of 2,000. If you can get a small concession of an MOQ of 1,800, you just lowered your inventory value by 10%, improved inventory turns, and freed up some extra cash. If you have a $10 million inventory, that's $1 million.

Deductions and claims – Hire a relentless bulldog to handle this area and you will no doubt save their salary many times over.

KEY POINT

Small incremental gains sometimes are more likely to be granted than large asks, and over enough transactions, that can lead to huge savings.

CHAPTER 8

WRITE YOURSELF A MEMO

Years ago, I had promoted a VP Sales and Marketing to the position of Managing Director of our Canadian division. It was his first time with this level of responsibility, and he wanted to do a great job. He asked me for guidance or anything he could keep in mind to help him get started. Below is a condensed version of what I sent him. He wound up doing a spectacular job in his new position, and I would rehire him in a heartbeat if the opportunity presented itself.

By the way, 15 years after I sent him the list, he tells me he still has a copy of that recap.

Memo To Self

1. Learn how to manage your boss. If you don't, your time and focus will be at his mercy and you will never be in control of your time.

2. Understand the basics of each operation that reports to you. Develop "flash reports" to track the basics so you can address problems early on.

3. Assess your organization. The wrong structure or wrong team is the kiss of death.

4. Build YOUR team.

5. Develop and communicate your expectations.

6. Develop a set of annual priorities by department that you review with each department monthly. Use dates and quantify expected results.

7. Walk around your building. Talk to people at all levels. They will tell you what is and isn't working.

8. Don't avoid problems, look for them; once you find them, you can fix them.

9. Be slow to commit and fast to deliver.

10. Post results everywhere. Treat it as everyone's report card.

11. Poor performance should have immediate consequences.

12. Weed out negative people.

13. Develop your replacement so you can move up.

14. Never let your boss be surprised; otherwise, controlling the reaction is unpredictable.

15. Treat everyone with respect. Don't let the people you don't like know it. No sense turning them against you.

16. Never kill the messenger.

17. Push decisions down, force your people to think and act. If they make wrong decisions, it tells you they are in the wrong position.

18. Deal with facts over opinions.

19. Keep your sense of humor.

20. Recognize and reward success quickly; go out of your way to do so.

21. Evaluate the upside potential and downside risk to your decisions.

22. Keep an even keel in good times and bad.

23. Follow up like a maniac. Set due dates so projects don't drift.

24. Focus on and reinforce a limited number of priorities at any one time.

25. Push product development. You either have unique product, a strong brand, or a patented process. Otherwise, you are competing on price.

26. Seek a long-term, sustainable, competitive advantage.

27. Monkeys—prepare your sales presentations with such clarity and data that anyone could present the program. Don't rely on the super salesmen idea.

28. Negotiate like crazy and understand the details of your product cost.

29. Treat the company's money like your own.

30. Set up authority levels so people know what they can and can't do.

31. Make sure your staff knows that good news needs to travel fast and bad news even faster.

32. Have fun.

About the Author

Robert Varakian has been president and CEO of some of the leading housewares and tabletop companies in the industry. In addition to managing the largest bakeware and cutlery supplier companies in the United States, he has created and launched several new brands. He has personally developed and introduced hundreds of products that have done hundreds of millions of dollars in sales. He has also been listed on numerous patents.

People who have worked with and for Bob have had this to say:

"Throughout a long career, you can expect to meet only a handful of people whose leadership will truly motivate and impact you over time. Bob Varakian is one of those leaders."

Marta Phillips, Group Marketing Manager, Hamilton Beach.

"Bob quickly became a mentor who stands to this day, and he developed me into the executive I am today. He has a knack for putting people in the right seats on the bus and steering that bus down the right road."

Chris Liccardi, COO, Flowater.

"Simply put, Bob is the most prolific product development person that I have worked with in my career."

Matthew Jones, Chief Commercial Officer, Mackenzie Childs.

"Bob is the best at product development and bringing new products to market."

Carolyn LeFavour, SVP sales, Lifetime Brands

"Bob has great vision for brand growth, a knack for working with people, and a roll up your sleeves approach to getting things done."

Lou Henry, Owner, A2 designs.

"Bob is a driving force in elevating business and brands strategically with design."

Steve Cozzolino, Cozzolino Studio.

"Bob is a true leader because he cares about his team; most of all, Bob is a teacher."

George Arnold, Director Global sourcing and supply, Ekco Housewares.

"Bob is simply the hardest working person I've ever had the distinction of working with."

Sid Ramarace, Corporate Strategy and Product Development.

Reference List

Burtt, Ben. 1992. *The American Gangster*. United States: Sony Pictures Home Entertainment.

Chase, David. 1999. *The Sopranos*. United States: Warner Bros. Television.

Coppola, Francis Ford, Nino Rota, and Carlo Savina. 1974. *The Godfather PART II*. United States: Paramount Pictures.

Coppola, Francis Ford. 1972. *The Godfather*. United States: Paramount Pictures.

Coppola, Francis Ford. 1990. *The Godfather Part III*. United States : Paramount Pictures.

DePalma, Brian. 1987. *The Untouchables*. United States: Paramount Pictures.

Devito, Danny. 1992. *Hoffa*. United States: 20th Century Fox.

Harmon, Robert. 1996. *Gotti*. United States: HBO.

Newell, Mike. 1997. *Donnie Brasco*. United States: TriStar Pictures.

Puzo, Mario. 1996. *The Last Don*. United States: Random House.

Scorsese, Martin. 1995. *Casino*. United States: Universal Pictures.

Sifakis, Carl. 1999. *The Mafia Encyclopedia*. United States: Checkmark Books.

Soderberg, Steven. 2001. *Oceans Eleven*. United States: Warner Bros. Pictures.

Tarantino, Quentin. 1994. *Pulp Fiction*. United States: Miramax.